T0328684

Cambridge Elements

Elements in Second Language Acquisition
edited by
Alessandro Benati
The University of Hong Kong
John W. Schwieter
Wilfrid Laurier University, Ontario

EXPLICIT AND IMPLICIT LEARNING IN SECOND LANGUAGE ACQUISITION

Bill VanPatten
Independent Scholar
Megan Smith
Mississippi State University

CAMBRIDGE
UNIVERSITY PRESS

CAMBRIDGE
UNIVERSITY PRESS

University Printing House, Cambridge CB2 8BS, United Kingdom

One Liberty Plaza, 20th Floor, New York, NY 10006, USA

477 Williamstown Road, Port Melbourne, VIC 3207, Australia

314–321, 3rd Floor, Plot 3, Splendor Forum, Jasola District Centre,
New Delhi – 110025, India

103 Penang Road, #05–06/07, Visioncrest Commercial, Singapore 238467

Cambridge University Press is part of the University of Cambridge.

It furthers the University's mission by disseminating knowledge in the pursuit of
education, learning, and research at the highest international levels of excellence.

www.cambridge.org
Information on this title: www.cambridge.org/9781009044325
DOI: 10.1017/9781009043571

First published 2022

A catalogue record for this publication is available from the British Library.

ISBN 978-1-009-04432-5 Paperback
ISSN 2517-7974 (online)
ISSN 2517-7966 (print)

Explicit and Implicit Learning in Second Language Acquisition

Elements in Second Language Acquisition

DOI: 10.1017/9781009043571
First published online: May 2022

Bill VanPatten
Independent Scholar

Megan Smith
Mississippi State University

Author for correspondence: Bill VanPatten, aliasbvp@gmail.com

Abstract: This Element explores the roles of explicit and implicit learning in second language acquisition. The authors lay out some key issues that they take to underlie the debate on the extent to which second language acquisition involves explicit learning, implicit learning, or both. They also discuss what they take to be an oversight in the field, namely the lack of clear definitions of key constructs. Taking a generative perspective on the nature of language, while addressing alternative approaches at key points, they refocus the discussion of explicit and implicit learning by first asking what must be learned (i.e., what is this mental representation we call "language" that all functioning humans possess?) The discussion and research reviewed leads to the conclusion that second language acquisition is largely if not exclusively implicit in nature and that explicit learning plays a secondary role in how learners grapple with meaning.

Keywords: explicit learning, implicit learning, second language acquisition, explicit knowledge, implicit knowledge

ISBNs: 9781009044325 (PB), 9781009043571 (OC)
ISSNs: 2517-7974 (online), 2517-7966 (print)

Contents

1 Introduction

There is a fundamental question underlying second language (L2) acquisition since the inception of the field in the late 1960s and early 1970s: To what extent are first language (L1) and L2 acquisition similar? Part of this question is the extent to which L2 learning is explicit. A key role for explicit learning would point to a fundamental difference between L1 and L2 acquisition because researchers generally agree that children acquiring their L1 engage implicit learning processes. That is, children don't think about what they're learning; they don't consciously go about trying to learn grammar, sounds, words, and so on. In a certain sense, acquisition just happens to them as a by-product of their communicative interactions with the world around them.

On the other hand, it is a general belief (among teachers, laypeople, and some researchers) that L2 learners, especially adolescents and adults, must somehow engage explicit learning processes in order to acquire language. That is, they must consciously focus on grammar, sounds, and words in order to "internalize" language. However, others disagree with this general belief. The purpose of the present Element is to review some of the issues that are central to the conflicting ideas about explicit and implicit learning processes in L2 acquisition. It is our contention that the evidence weighs heavily on the side of implicit learning in L2 acquisition and that much of the debate about explicit and implicit learning involves problems in definitions of key constructs, methodological issues in research, and what one might consider not seeing the forest for the trees (i.e., there is some evidence that has been staring researchers in the face all along but gets ignored as researchers focus only on micro-studies conducted in laboratories).

The Element is divided into the following major sections:

- definitions and explication of key constructs, namely what learning is, what language is, and what acquisition is (Section 2);
- three possible positions: (1) L2 acquisition is largely or exclusively explicit in nature; (2) L2 acquisition is largely or exclusively implicit; (3) L2 acquisition involves both implicit and explicit learning (Section 3);
- whether or not explicit knowledge can become implicit knowledge (Section 4); and
- issues that confound the conclusions from such as noticing, laboratory research, Poverty of the Stimulus, and other approaches (i.e., approaches to the nature of language that are different from ours) (Section 5).

Finally, in Section 6 we offer concluding remarks and briefly touch on the relevance of the explicit/implicit learning issue for practitioners.

2 First, Some Definitions

2.1 Explicit and Implicit Learning

Learning is the internalization of some kind of data or information from the environment. The internalization of such data causes a change in an internal cognitive structure (e.g., VanPatten & Rothman, 2014). This definition is important as later we will enter into a discussion of the possibility that some aspects of language aren't learned at all; they fall out of what has been called the "human language faculty." In other words, some aspects of language aren't learned explicitly or implicitly because they are not internalized from the environment. In these cases, however, the processes by which such aspects of language get triggered are, by definition, implicit in nature.

Historically, L2 scholars have distinguished between explicit and implicit learning largely due to Reber's work on the primacy of implicit learning beginning in the 1960s (e.g., Reber, 1967). Well-known to scholars in this area, Reber examined how participants faired on a test of "grammaticality" after being exposed to strings of letters developed by what was called a Markovian Chain or a finite-state grammar. Sample strings of letters include TXS, TSXS, TSSXXVV, TSXXTVPS, PVV, PTTVPSPTVPXVPS, and PTVPXVPS. After exposure, participants judged both previously viewed and novel strings as to whether they were possible or not. Reber's conclusion (subsequently challenged but later supported) was that participants learn the "rules" of the finite-state grammar implicitly, as they were largely unable to say why strings of letters were grammatical or ungrammatical.

Interestingly, Reber did not actually define implicit learning directly in his original publications, instead referring vaguely to something that resembled statistical tallying (e.g., Ellis & Wulff, 2015; Rebuschat, 2015). It was not until 1993 that we find a definition: "Implicit learning is the acquisition of knowledge that takes place largely independently of conscious attempts to learn and largely in the absence of explicit knowledge about what was acquired" (Reber, 1993, p. 5).[1] In Reber's thinking, then, implicit learning is defined in opposition to explicit learning. Reber began examining explicit learning in 1976. Much like his early work on implicit learning, he did not define explicit learning but instead operationalized it by including an "explicit group" of participants who were given instructions to actively search for rules that underlay the array of letters generated by a finite-state grammar. The explicit group in this study was

---

[1] Reber (1976) still does not define implicit learning directly but does say that "Implicit learning has been characterized as a process whereby a subject becomes sensitive to the structure inherent in a complex array by developing (implicitly) a conceptual model which reflects the structure to some degree" (p. 88). For additional discussion, see the various papers in Underwood (1996).

given the following directions as part of the experimental treatment: "[I]t will be to your advantage if you can figure out what the rules are, which letters may follow other letters and which ones may not. Such knowledge will certainly help you in learning and memorizing the items" (Reber, 1976, p. 89). Thus, explicit learning under this scenario seems to mean a conscious intent to discern patterns or rules in some kind of input.[2] Implicit learning, then, would be learning something without the intent to do so.

In L2 research, definitions of explicit and implicit learning vary somewhat but essentially capture Reber's ideas. We offer examples from three exemplary essays on the nature of L2 learning:[3]

> Implicit learning is acquisition of knowledge about the underlying structure of a complex stimulus environment by a process which takes place naturally, simply and without conscious operations. Explicit learning is a more conscious operation where the individual makes and tests hypotheses in a search for structure. (Ellis, 1994a, p. 1)

> Explicit learning is input processing with the conscious intention to find out whether the input information contains regularities and, if so, to work out the concepts and rules with which these regularities can be captured. Implicit learning is input processing without such an intention, taking place unconsciously. (Hulstijn, 2005, p. 131)

> Implicit learning, essentially the process of acquiring unconscious (implicit) knowledge, is a fundamental feature of human cognition ... explicit learning refers to a process during which participants acquire conscious (explicit) knowledge; this is generally associated with intentional learning conditions ... (Rebuschat, 2015, p. xiii)

It seems, then, that, irrespective of one's theoretical orientation (e.g., VanPatten, Keating, & Wulff, 2020), the difference between explicit and implicit learning hinges largely on intent. That is, explicit learning involves some kind of intent to purposefully learn something, whereas, with implicit learning, there is no such intent (see also Williams, 2009). *Intent* can be one's own intent or be externally induced through what Reber calls an "instructional set." For our purposes, it's important to note that, with the possible exceptions of skill-theoretical and sociocultural approaches to Second Language Acquisition (SLA), all current discussions on adult L2 learning posit input as a necessary condition; that is,

---

[2] The use of "some kind of input" is purposeful here as few would claim that the kind of input used in Reber's research could be considered the kind of linguistic input as normally conceived in first and second language acquisition. Finite-state grammars are not "grammars" and letter strings are not "sentences" as commonly defined by linguists that encode not just formal properties but also meaning. For discussion, see VanPatten (1994).

[3] For additional definitions and commentary on these constructs, see DeKeyser (2003).

they all agree that language acquisition does not happen in the absence of input. Thus, the definitions of explicit and implicit learning ought to be tied directly to how learners engage input as they encounter it within communicative or meaningful events (see the above-cited quote from Hulstijn, 2005).

As we will see in Section 5.3, in applied L2 research on explicit and implicit learning, Reber's original idea is sometimes distorted. In Reber's research, explicit and implicit groups only differed in that the explicit group was told to search for patterns but, crucially, they were never told what the patterns were ahead of time. As such, they were left to their own devices to try to come up with them. In L2 research, we sometimes see this operationalization of explicit/implicit, but we also see others, making the research messy and often a problem of comparing apples to oranges. In such research, the construct of "explicit" is operationalized as an explanation or description of a "rule" or "form" and can be followed by exposure to stimuli or some kind of actual practice (in the traditional sense of practice). In other words, explicit teaching and practice are conflated with explicit learning (i.e., there was no explicit teaching or practice in Reber's foundational work). In this Element, we are focused on what learners do with input as they are exposed to it, not on what learners do in response to explicit teaching and practice. In this sense, explicit learning might be conceived of as explicit processing of input. In other words, explicit learning is input processing with the intention to search for rules or regularities in the input.

Although such definitions are clearly important for matters such as operationalization during empirical research, they are equally important for the constructs embedded within them – especially those that are not defined. In the particular case of explicit and implicit learning in L2 research (as well as the field of cognitive psychology), we note that definitions of explicit and implicit learning almost always contain constructs such as "rules," "knowledge," and "structure." Such constructs clearly are meant to refer to language, but, interestingly, no characterization of language is offered in any research on the explicit and implicit learning of languages (that is, that we can find). Just what do researchers mean by "rules," "knowledge," "structure," or any other term used in discussions about explicit and implicit learning? Is there some common definition of language that underlies the research in this area? What is it, exactly, that researchers believe learners are constructing as linguistic systems? In anticipation of the ideas we will develop in this Element, we see the nature of language as fundamental to the discussion of explicit and implicit learning, for without a characterization of the "implicit knowledge" that learners are supposed to acquire, researchers may at best be talking past each other or, at worst, arguing over something that turns out not to be grounded in the nature of language. We turn our attention now to a characterization of language we will use in this Element. In Section 5.1, we will briefly review some alternatives to this characterization.

2.2 Language

Language is distinct from communication. Language is an abstract, complex, and implicit system of mental representations. It is generative and creative in nature, meaning that whatever exists within this system generates all utterances and can create utterances a speaker has not heard, read, said, or written before. In contrast, communication is the expression and interpretation of meaning in a given (social) context for a particular purpose. For most humans, language is a principal tool – albeit not the only one – used in communication. Thus, the learner may draw upon language to communicate – read a newspaper or novel, watch a TV show or movie, or participate in a conversation, for example – but such activities are not the linguistic system itself. Thus, when we talk about language acquisition, we don't have communication in mind, important though it is. Rather, what we have in mind is the underlying mental representation that may be tapped during communication.

The linguistic system is modular and it includes a number of subsystems – the most researched include the lexicon, the morphological system, the syntactic component, and the phonological system. What gets acquired, then, are elements of these modules as well as the ways in which they interact with each other.

2.2.1 The Lexicon

Although this is an imperfect analogy, the lexicon is essentially a mental dictionary in that it contains information about words and morphemes. Morphemes are the smallest units of meaning in any given language, so all words consist of at least one morpheme, but not all morphemes are words. The lexicon stores individual morphemes, not words, so this is one way in which the analogy of a dictionary breaks down. Another way in which the analogy breaks down is that the lexicon is organized by both frequency and similarity, with connections between morphemes based on phonological and/or semantic similarity, and more frequently used morphemes are more easily accessed than less frequently used morphemes. Words and morphemes are stored with the following information: phonological form, semantic representation, features, and co-occurrence information. Let's consider the lexical entry in (1):[4]

---

[4] This notational structure for lexical entries comes from Carnie (2011). There are other approaches to the lexicon, but they all share these same basic elements. Nothing we discuss in what follows hinges on this particular analysis.

(1)   *Dog*

$$
\begin{bmatrix}
\text{PF[d}\alpha\text{g]} \\
\text{CATEGORY} \begin{bmatrix} \text{N} \\ \text{[+ count]} \end{bmatrix} \\
\text{ARG} - \varphi \begin{bmatrix} \text{PERS} & 3 \\ \text{[NUM} & 1] \end{bmatrix} \\
\text{SEM} \quad \text{[dog]}
\end{bmatrix}
$$

This lexical entry contains the following information: phonological form (PF), that is, the information about how the word is pronounced; information about which syntactic category the word belongs to; agreement features (listed here as AGR-φ features); and the word's meaning. So, this lexical entry is pronounced [dɑg], is a count noun (which has consequences for which determiners it can co-occur with), and is a third-person, singular noun. All of this is information that the syntax will make use of.

The lexical entry in (1) is for *dog*, which is a noun. This entry therefore includes information relevant to nouns, including agreement features for person and number and whether the noun is a mass noun or a count noun. Lexical entries for verbs include information relevant to verbs, namely the argument or arguments that the verb takes and whether those arguments are optional. Much like the lexical entries for nouns and verbs, functional categories, such as determiners and tense, also have lexical entries. The lexical entry for tense, for example, includes features that ensure that the verb gets marked for tense and the appropriate auxiliary verb is selected and that the subject of the sentence gets marked for nominative case.

In short, all of the information the syntax needs to combine one lexical entry with another to form a multi-word phrase is stored with each lexical entry. Some of this information is fairly straightforward, such as the word's syntactic category and its pronunciation. Some of this is far more abstract, such as a word's agreement features and what it co-occurs with (for instance, its internal and external arguments or its theta grid). And, in some cases, we have lexical entries that are purely abstract, such as those for Tense. These abstract entries play a vitally important role. Including a lexical entry for Tense, for instance, ensures that every sentence has Tense, and because Tense is the mechanism by which nominative case is checked, it also ensures that every sentence has a subject. In other words, these abstract categories are, in many ways, the "glue" that binds sentences together and makes sure they are all grammatical for a particular language.

2.2.2 Syntax

Syntax is the linguistic module or subsystem that combines words into phrases and phrases into sentences. It is a computational system and uses just a few operations to combine lexical entries into phrases and sentences. These basic operations are universal in that they operate in all of the world's languages. In addition to these basic operations, syntax also includes linguistic universals and language-specific constraints that (1) are learned or derived from the input and (2) interact with universal operations to construct phrases and sentences. Today, the set of linguistic universals and language-specific constraints is thought to be significantly smaller than it was in the early years of linguistic theory. These universals include the inventory of syntactic categories, the stipulation that these categories must be organized with respect to each other in some way (i.e., phrase structure rules), and the requirement that every sentence has a subject and a set of features (e.g., Case, Tense, person/number/gender agreement, and so forth). Several of these universals have options associated with them, such that, for instance, every language must order key elements with respect to each other, but each language is free to choose how it orders them. This universal paired with this option gives us SOV languages like Japanese, Korean, Latin, and Turkish; SVO languages like English, French, Spanish, and Mandarin; and VSO languages like Irish, Welsh, and Hawaiian. Similarly, although every sentence is required to have a subject, this subject can be obligatorily overt, such as in English and French, or optionally (and sometimes obligatorily) null, such as in Korean and Italian. These language-specific constraints on how universals are realized are, coupled with phonological and lexical differences, a primary source of linguistic diversity.

In addition to these language-level constraints, the syntax also contains a set of operations that allows words to be combined into phrases and sentences. These operations are Merge, Move, and Agree. Merge combines two lexical entries into a phrase. Merge can only combine lexical entries whose feature structures match – this is why the lexicon stores this information – which means, for instance, that Merge cannot combine the verb *chase* with a complementizer phrase (CP) because *chase* cannot select a CP as its internal or external argument. Move allows phrases to move from one position in the sentence to another. For example, the *wh-* question *What did you eat?* involves moving *what*, which is the object of the verb *eat*, to the beginning of the sentence to form a question. As an operation, however, Move is somewhat constrained. It can only operate to satisfy features, such as Case features or question features. Agree is another feature-checking operation, but it functions at more local levels and ensures that feature structures are compatible once Merge has taken place.

Syntax is an abstract system, and this abstraction sometimes strikes people as implausible because it seems like the abstract nature of the system makes it difficult, or impossible, to acquire. However, most of this system is "hardwired" as part of the human capacity for language. Of the elements discussed in this section, the only parts of the syntax that must be acquired on the basis of input are language-specific constraints such as word order and whether the language permits null subjects and the specific features that a language instantiates (e.g., not all languages instantiate Case or do so the same way). These features are mapped to lexical entries, so the acquisition of syntax is a by-product of lexical learning. The basics of the computational system are built into the human capacity for language, and language-specific instances of movement and agreement are acquired as a result of acquiring individual features. We will return to this issue in Sections 2.3 and 4.

2.2.3 Phonology

A third linguistic module that must be acquired is phonology. Phonology includes the set of sounds a given language makes use of, the rules for combining these sounds, and suprasegmental information such as stress, intonation contours, and the ability to identify word boundaries. Because the set of possible sounds in human language is finite, it is likely that a second language learner will already be able to produce and perceive some of the sounds in the target language because they are instantiated in the learner's first language. The nature of the phonological learning task, however, depends to a large extent on what the phonological inventories of the learner's L1 and L2 look like. For example, the phonological inventory of Standard American English consists of the following consonants: [p] [b] [m] [f] [v] [θ] [ð] [t] [d] [n] [s] [z] [l] [ɹ] [ʃ] [ʒ] [tʃ] [dʒ] [j] [k] [g] [ŋ] [h] [w]. This means that a native American English speaker will perceive each of these sounds as distinct from each other and will also perceive them in other languages. English has a relatively large array of consonants, including several (e.g., [f] [v] [θ] [ð]) that are relatively rare cross-linguistically. A native speaker of Japanese has a language whose phonological inventory includes the consonants [p] [b] [ɸ] [s] [ss] [z] [t] [tt] [d] [r] [n] [m] [j] [w] [k] [kk] [g]. The L1 Japanese speaker learning English, then, has to learn to perceive several new sounds, some of which, such as [ʃ] and [tʃ], are allophones of the phonemes [s] and [t] in Japanese. Because English has a larger phonological inventory than Japanese does, Japanese learners of English must learn to perceive more sounds than English learners of Japanese do. That said, Japanese also has sounds, such as geminate consonants, that English lacks and English learners of Japanese must learn to perceive these sounds. These are examples of phonological learning at the segmental level; learners must also acquire suprasegmental features such as stress, pitch, and intonation contours. The phonological learning task may seem monumental, but, as we will see in Section 2.3, the main driver of acquisition is communicatively embedded input, and phonemes make a meaningful difference in a given language.

2.3 Acquisition

Holding social context constant,[5] we build upon mainstream approaches in that there are three principal ingredients that interact to shape language in the learner's mind/brain: (1) input, (2) internal mechanisms that constrain and contribute to the shape of language, and (3) processors that mediate between input and the internal mechanisms.[6] The nature of input is relatively uncontroversial, so we will dispense with it quickly. Input (also called "primary linguistic data") consists of language that learners hear (or see) that is embedded in a communicative event. That is, the role of learners is to interpret the meaning encoded in the language they are exposed to. Thus, input is language intended for learner comprehension of some kind of message.

We take the internal mechanisms to be of two types. The first are mechanisms that are language-specific. The second are those that are learning-general. The major language-specific mechanism we have in mind is Universal Grammar (UG), whose principal function is to restrict the nature of language as it grows in the mind/brain. Under current accounts of linguistic theory (i.e., Minimalism; see, e.g., Hornstein, Nunes, & Grohmann, 2005, as well as the collection in Boeckx, 2011), the content of UG is both agreed on and debated. Important for the present discussion is what is agreed on. Common to all current conceptualizations, UG consists of an inventory of features (e.g., Case, Aspect, Tense, Question), some principles (e.g., phrase structure), and basic operations (e.g., Merge/Move, Agree). Thus, as we saw in Sections 2.2.1 and 2.2.2, sentence structure is the result of a complex interaction of phrase structure, computations involving movement, and agreement based on features encoded in the syntax and the lexicon.

The second set of internal mechanisms includes those that are responsible for general learning and data processing, including those that tabulate frequency. So, while UG restricts the basic properties or nature of language, the general learning mechanisms are partly responsible for which features make it into the developing system more quickly than others and how robustly they are

---

[5] By holding social context constant, we acknowledge that it plays a role in both the quantity and the quality of interactions that learners receive in the L2 (e.g., VanPatten, Smith, & Benati, 2020). This role affects progress, ultimate attainment, attitudes, and other matters that form the complex quilt that is adult SLA. However, for the present discussion on input and internal mechanisms, social context plays no discernible role.

[6] Readers familiar with the Modular Online Growth and Use of Language (MOGUL) might see some similarity in our discussion here with that framework (see, e.g., Sharwood Smith & Truscott, 2014).

represented in the lexicon (for a more extended discussion, see Sharwood Smith & Truscott, 2014, as well as Yang, 2004). As a simple illustration, if a language selects for the abstract feature Tense (i.e., finiteness), then that feature must be represented in the morpho-syntax somehow. In Spanish, for example, it is represented in verbal morphology and in word order that is the result of movement to check Tense or Question features. The general learning mechanisms are not responsible for learning about movement and feature checking, but they are implicated in the acquisition of, for instance, verbal morphology that includes Tense features. As discussed in Section 2.2.2, syntactic movement happens in order to check features, so acquiring these features will result in acquiring movement operations as well.

Generally left out of the discussion in L2 research but worth mentioning here is that language acquisition also makes use of those mechanisms that aid in discerning meaning – possibly related to general learning mechanisms. By this we mean that, as learners process language, they are also engaged in figuring out what an input string means or what a particular word or phrase means. Such mechanisms are unspecified in the literature on SLA, but the field may wish to consider these mechanisms more closely as they may be an important aspect of explicit learning related to nonformal elements of language.

Between the input "out there" and the mechanisms "somewhere inside" is another mechanism or set of mechanisms that bridges the two. These are called "input processors." In other words, UG does not directly make use of input but instead makes use of processed input data (e.g., VanPatten, 1996; VanPatten & Rothman, 2014). These data are, essentially (but not exclusively), what we call form-meaning connections and consist largely of morphophonological units, that is, words and their inflections as well as chunks of language used in formulaic utterances (e.g., "Howzitgoin?" "Whatsup?"). An example of variation among form-meaning connections would be the Spanish verb *escribo* "I write/I'm writing" versus *escribe* "he wrote." Each would, if tagged for encoded information, look like this:

(2) *escribo* ["write" + thematic grid] [−N] [+V] [+PRESENT] [−PAST] [+1st] [−PL] [−PERFECTIVE], and so on

(3) *escribe* ["write" + thematic grid] [−N] [+V] [−PRESENT] [+PAST] [−PL] [+PERFECTIVE], and so on

For a variety of reasons beyond the scope of the present discussion (but see, e.g., VanPatten, 1996, 2015), learners do not necessarily tag each and every morphophonological unit in the input with meaning, nor do they tag each morphophonological unit with its full meaning. What is more, the strength of the encoded information for the morphophonological unit is partially determined by frequency in the input. So, the more times the learner encounters, say, *escribo* in the input and properly links it to the speaker's reference to his/her own writing, the greater the chances are that, over time, all of the underlying features will get encoded and will be robustly represented in the lexical entry. Thus, the processing and learning of morphophonological units involve the mapping of both meaning *and* grammatical properties onto the units and storing them in the lexicon along with a relative index of strength or robustness (again, see also Sharwood Smith & Truscott, 2014). Morphological features such as verb endings are subsequently derived from the hundreds of encounters of verbs in the input that share a morphological ending. Thus, for example in Spanish, repeated exposure to verbs such as *escribo* "I write," *tomo* "I take," *vivo* "I live," and numerous others results in the learner unconsciously incorporating into the lexicon the specific features associated with the -*o* ending that mark specific features (such as present tense and first-person singular). Thus, over time, a separate lexical entry for -*o* is developed even though the lexicon may retain the original examples of *escribo, tomo, vivo,* and others in their entirety.

At the same time, the learner's parser must build a syntactic representation of the sentence encountered. Parsing entails moment-by-moment computations of structural relationships among phrases while at the same time projecting those same phrases as words are encountered. This process involves universal strategies, language-specific information, possibly L1 parsing routines (i.e., transfer during processing), and general strategies of "filling in" and "guessing" depending on the level of the learner and individual differences. Minimally, the parser determines what the verb is, what noun phrases there are, and what the relationships of these noun phrases are to the verb (e.g., which is the subject, if any; which is an object, if any) and to any other phrases. The parser also determines the overall hierarchical relationship among the phrases.

With these ideas in mind, we can illustrate with an example from Spanish. The early-stage learner encounters the following during a communicative exchange: *¿Dónde viven tus padres?* "Where do your parents live?" The eventual knowledge that must form part of the underlying mental representation consists of, among other things, the following:[7]

- *donde* ["where"] [+LOC] [+Q]
- *viven* ["live" + thematic grid] [−N] [+V] [+PRESENT] [−PAST] [+3rd] [+PL] [−PERFECTIVE]
- *tus* ["your"] [+D] [+SPECIFIC] [+2nd] [NUM:−PL] [AGR:+PL]
- *padres* ["parents"] [+N] [−V] [+3rd] [+PL]
- copy of *wh-* element to CP and deletion in VP

---

[7] For the purposes of illustration, we have not included the phonological features in these examples.

- copy of V to AgrP and deletion in VP
- copy of V to T and deletion in AgrP
- copy of N to [Spec, TP] and deletion in VP

The beginning learner will not make all of the connections during initial and subsequent input processing, although it is likely that the operations will be flagged and encoded as the sentence is computed. That is, it is likely that the parser correctly delivers linear information on word order such that the internal mechanisms "make note" that the *wh-* element and the V are not in their canonical places (i.e., the V does not appear after the subject NP as expected and a locative phrase does not appear after the verb as expected), laying the groundwork for the representation that there is both *wh-* and verb movement in this language. The connections likely not made during the initial stages of processing are the [+3rd] [+PL] of the V element and the [+PL] of the D element, for example, such that what the learner encodes at this initial stage of processing is *viven* ["live"] [+V] [+PRESENT] [−PAST] and *tus* ["your"] [+D] [+SPECIFIC] [+2nd]. The missing underlying features (in this case, Number) are provided by the morphophonological unit *padres* and are recoverable there (i.e., the Lexical Preference Principle; see, for example, VanPatten, 2004, 2020).

Again, this simple example assumes successful overall comprehension of the sentence; that is, it assumes that the learner understands that someone is asking where his/her parents live. It is possible that processing and sentence building might not be successful because comprehension of an utterance is not successful. For example, what if a learner is encountering a word for the first time or has yet to attach meaning to a form previously encountered? In such cases, processing is delayed until subsequent encounters in the input and the learner can figure meaning out on his/her own. Or, negotiation of meaning may occur on the spot, such that processing can happen piecemeal during the exchange. Once more, we offer a simple example (I = interlocutor, L = learner).

(4)   I: ¿Dónde viven tus padres?
        L: ¿Vi-vi-viven?
        I: Sí, sí. ¿Dónde viven? ¿Viven en Michigan? ¿Viven en Ohio?
        L: Oh! Oh! Viven! You're asking me where they live. Uh, en Michigan. En Grand Rapids.

In this interchange, pieces and parts of the original utterance get processed over time. In the first pass, the learner may understand that a question is being asked (projecting a CP with a [+Q] feature into the syntactic computation) and has penciled in major parts of the sentence (there is a *wh-* element in what must be the CP, there is a V in a position that must be higher than the TP, there is an NP that must be the subject NP and is probably in TP) but hasn't tagged the V with its meaning yet. It is not until the end of the interchange that the learner uncovers the meaning of the V element and can "insert" it into the utterance to complete the sentence structure initiated during the first pass.

Before continuing, we offer one more example. This time, let's imagine the early-stage learner encounters something like the following during an interchange: *No quiere ir a Chile* "He doesn't want to go to Chile." This example involves something a bit different because of the presence of a null element in the sentence (i.e., Spanish is a null-subject language that licenses/requires null-subject pronouns under various conditions). The sentence contains a *pro* as the subject of *quiere* "wants," and for the purposes of the present discussion, we are going to focus on this element and ignore the processing of the others. A null element like *pro* has no phonetic content, unlike the morphophonological units seen so far and unlike its explicit counterpart, *él* "he." At the same time, the learner has to process this sentence by attributing subject status to something, as mandated by the Extended Projection Principle (i.e., all finite sentences must have a subject), and to make sure the theta grid (i.e., entities required by the semantics of the verb) is complete, as described in Pritchett (1992). That is, the processor wants to tag something as the subject of the sentence so that the sentence parse is successful. In this particular case, by the time the learner gets to the end of the sentence no possible NP is found that can serve the role of subject (i.e., "Chile" is ruled out because it is denoted as part of the [+LOC] feature within the PP needed to fulfill the requirements of the phrase *ir a* "go to." In such a scenario, the parser/processor can posit an empty category to "fill in" for the subject NP position of the sentence and the learner's internal mechanisms begin to instantiate "null subjectness" for the language being learned. Repeated encounters of this sort reinforce the idea of null subjectness; thus *pro* is confirmed as an entry in the lexicon/grammar and all relevant (universal) properties of null-subject languages are triggered.

From this brief description of acquisition, there are three things happening during real-time acquisition-as-processing worth underscoring. One is that the learner must uncover the meaning and intent of the other interlocutor. That is, as in the negotiated interaction presented in (4) above, the learner must arrive at what the speaker is attempting to communicate. The second is that the morphophonological units within the input stream must be isolated and tagged with meaning, including the underlying features that form part of the meaning. Thus, we have meaning processing at the broader level (i.e., What is this person saying to me?), meaning at the morphophonological level (i.e., What does this particular word or unit mean?), and then there is meaning expressed within particular kinds of underlying features (e.g., [TENSE], [PERSON], [NUMBER]). As a preview to our argument in the next section, it is likely that learners engage explicit processes to uncover meaning at the broader level but not for the underlying features associated with meaning at the morphophonological level. Finally, the third thing happening during real-time acquisition is that learners must compute sentence structure at a fairly abstract level that includes not only categories of words and where they are in a sentence but also whether movement and agreement have occurred.

To summarize, acquisition is comprehension-dependent in that the primary data for acquisition reside in the communicatively embedded input that learners are exposed to. Internal mechanisms select and operate on data over time, making use of both language-specific and general learning mechanisms to tag, organize, and store linguistic data. Much of what is tagged, organized, and stored involves highly abstract concepts and features that interact in complex ways.

3 So, Where Does This Leave Us with the Explicit/Implicit Debate?

Given the discussion thus far, we can now look at three possibilities for explicit and implicit learning in L2 research.

- The linguistic system is learned explicitly.
- The linguistic system is learned implicitly.
- The linguistic system is learned both explicitly and implicitly.

3.1 Language Is Learned (Only or Largely) Explicitly

The first possibility is ruled out. Given the nature of language outlined here, it is highly unlikely, if not impossible, that learners intentionally go about trying to uncover abstract features in the input such as Tense, Case and Question. Similarly, it is unlikely that learners go looking for operations such as Move and Agree, or that they are consciously aware of universals, such as phrase structure, or options in language, such as word order and null subjects. Analogously, although classroom instruction does tend to involve explicit attention to grammar explanations, these explanations do not involve the explicit teaching of features and operations. To a large extent, this is the domain of linguistics – and the existence of linguists who know a lot about the underlying systems of specific languages without being able to speak those languages provides some evidence that explicit attention to these underlying structures does not lead to language acquisition. Additionally, we cannot conceive of any way in which the implicit linguistic system as described in this Element can be learned explicitly. Learners may go about explicitly looking for how past tense is encoded on verb forms (e.g., "I think *spoke* means he did it yesterday") and in some laboratory experiments under so-called implicit conditions (see Section 5.3) participants sometimes (but not always and not often) report looking for things in the input. However, this is not the same thing as looking for Tense as a feature (e.g., "From this input this language must have the feature [+FINITE] so there must be at least a [+PRESENT] [−PRESENT] distinction. I'll be on the lookout."). Comprehension would come to a halt if learners had to explicitly code for abstract linguistic features as they processed input.

3.2 Language Is Learned (Only or Largely) Implicitly

The conclusion that explicit learning is not central or perhaps even possible in L2 acquisition leads us to the second possibility: The linguistic system – at least the formal linguistic system – is learned implicitly. This perspective is widely supported in the literature (see, e.g., the collections in Rebuschat, 2015; VanPatten, Keating, & Wulff, 2020). We do not base this conclusion on the explicit versus implicit learning conditions investigated in laboratory studies (which we will touch on in Section 5.3). Instead, we base this on the vast literature on how the learner's linguistic system evolves over time, research that has appeared since the outset of contemporary L2 research in the 1970s. We can illustrate with a simple example from a classic study on staged development: the acquisition of *ser* and *estar* in Spanish.

In Spanish, there are two verbs that are more or less equivalent to English "be" in function. They are *ser* and *estar*. Both can serve as copular verbs and as auxiliaries, just like "be," but they are not interchangeable. For example, *ser* can serve as a copular verb with NPs (e.g., *Bill es linguista* "Bill is a linguist") but not *estar* (e.g., **Bill está linguista*). *Ser* functions as an auxiliary in passives while *estar* does not (e.g., *Megan fue contratada* "Megan was hired"),[8] while *estar* functions as an auxiliary with progressives while *ser* does not (e.g., *Megan está escribiendo algo* "Megan is writing something"). Research over the years has shown that learners of Spanish go through at least four identifiable stages in the acquisition of these two verbs (see, e.g., the summary in VanPatten, 2010).

Stage 1: no verb. Learners simply omit the verb, as in *Kevin joven* "lit: Kevin young" and *María enferma* "lit: Mary sick."

---

[8] *Estar* can be used in stative passives to mean something different, as in *Megan está contratada*, which doesn't report on the act of her being hired but instead on the resultant state of her having a job.

Stage 2: *ser* emerges and takes over almost all functions of both verbs. *Kevin es joven* but also *María es enferma. Ella no es aquí* "Mary is sick. She's not here," *Paco es estudiando/Paco es estudiar* "Paco is studying," and so on.

Stage 3: *estar* emerges as an auxiliary and learners gain control of its use with progressives, as in *Paco está estudiando* "Paco is studying."

Stage 4: *estar* emerges as copular and learners gain control over its use with location and with adjectives, as in *María está enferma* "Mary is sick" and *Ella no está aquí* "She's not here."

The research is based on spontaneous speech and elicited conversational speech in which chunks and formulaic expressions are removed (e.g., routines such as *¿Cómo estás?* "How are you?" which tend to exist as one unanalyzed chunk), as well as other experimental methods (e.g., truth-value tasks, self-paced reading). Researchers have investigated the stages of development of Spanish copular verbs with learners from a variety of L1 backgrounds, including English, Chinese, and Korean. Because English has one verb for *be*, Korean has a copular verb that shares some (but not all) functions of English *be*, and Chinese has no such verb, the stages observed cannot be due to L1 influence.

What we wish to point out is that at each and every stage the learner is operating with an implicit representation for how Tense is represented in Spanish and what can be inserted to reflect this feature. Like most copular verbs, the Spanish verbs for "be" are basically meaningless. They carry no real-world meaning compared to verbs like "run," "spit," and "finish." They are required in Spanish to reflect Tense (like English) as well as person-number features (unlike English, although "be" is irregular and has three forms in the present tense). In Stage 1, learners have yet to consistently project Tense into the syntax, which is why we get sentences without copular and auxiliary verbs. This is consistent with other things they do such as a largely uneven ability to put person-number endings for present tense on verbs, often using "bare verbs" such as *corre* "run" and *estudia* "study" for most person-number situations (we'll see this in our second example).

One conclusion from such research is that Stage 1 reflects both an implicit system and implicit learning because (1) it does not resemble anything learners are taught (i.e., learners are not taught to leave out verbs), (2) it does not resemble what is available in the input (regular sentences in Spanish always have verbs and learners do hear, or read, copular and auxiliary *ser/estar* in the input), and (3) it does not look like English (so they aren't transferring a singular English "be" from the outset if that is their L1). Clearly, the system is not reflective of explicit or conscious rules. Instead, each and every stage in the acquisition of *ser* and *estar* reflects abstract properties of language that are involved in the implicit nature of that stage. Indeed, what this research suggests is that learners are unconsciously building a system over time in which the feature of [+/−PERFECTIVE] is mapped onto these verbs (e.g., Roby, 2007; Schmitt, 2005; VanPatten, 2010). This is not a feature that is explicitly taught to learners and we can't imagine a scenario where learners explicitly search for this feature in the input.

We offer a second and related example. Spanish is morphologically rich when it comes to verb endings. What follows are the person-number endings for present tense verbs.[9]

	SINGULAR	PLURAL
1ST	-o/ -oy	-mos
2ND	-s	-is
3RD	-a/-e	-n

To put the endings into something concrete, we illustrate with the verb *correr* "to run."

	SINGULAR	PLURAL
1ST	corro	corremos
2ND	corres	correis
3RD	corre	corren

In terms of the acquisition of person-number endings in L2 Spanish, we typically see the following in spontaneous and free communicative speech.

- First, learners use a bare verb and this generally is the same as third-person singular. This verb is "overgeneralized" to all person-number contexts (and even tenses). Example: *Yo no corre. No me gusta.* "I don't run. I don't like it."
- Second, we see the singulars emerge as learners gain control over them with the third-person singular no longer being a bare verb only but actually being more and more restricted to the third-person singular. Usually, the first singular emerges before the second singular. Example: *Yo no corro. ¿Tú corres?* "I don't run. Do you run?"
- Third, we see the plural forms emerge, and generally it is the third plural that emerges before the others.

Clearly these stages do not reflect instruction or explicit practice in any way (i.e., the present and practice of verb forms in Spanish classes are not ordered;

---

9 For historical reasons, non-peninsular dialects of Spanish use the third plural form of verbs for second plural and also use third singular for second singular for differential or "formal" address.

instead, learners get them all at once and work with them all at once) and they
don't reflect what is available in the input that learners might explicitly process.
Instead, they represent what is happening in the implicit system from the outset.
In Spanish, learners have to develop a new functional phrase in the syntax
labeled AGRP (Agreement Phrase). This phrase is nestled somewhere under the
Tense Phrase so that the underlying structure (with all other functional phrases
not present) looks like the structure in (5):

(5)

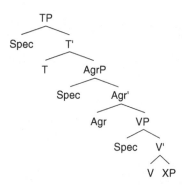

In Spanish, verbs have to move out of their place of origin, pass through Agr to
get person-number features checked, and wind up in T in regular declarative
sentences to get tense features checked. (We know this because of the various
word orders we get in Spanish and because we can test this with other languages
similar and dissimilar to Spanish.) This is what learners are headed toward. But,
clearly in the initial stage, learners have no agreement. Their implicit system is,
in essence, featureless when it comes to both Tense and Agreement. We might
even characterize it as something that looks like the structure in (6).

(6)

In other words, their initial representation is "bare bones." We are not
suggesting that this underlying structure is what is in the earliest stage of the
implicit system (some scholars have claimed it is; e.g., Vainikka & Young-
Scholten, 1996). What is clear is that learners are functioning with some kind of
implicit system or the first stage wouldn't consist of bare verbs like *corre*. As in

the case of *ser* and *estar*, this stage is not reflective of anything that learners are taught or that they learn explicitly. What is more, although we call third-person singular "third-person singular," standard analyses converge on the idea that this particular verb form in Spanish is actually featureless. It is neither third nor singular and doesn't indicate any person or number (although technically it does carry TENSE as a feature). Learners seem to have this implicit representation; that is, that something like *corre* is featureless (bare). Therefore, it can be used in almost any context without "agreement clash" (e.g., McCarthy, 2006; see also Alemán Bañón, Miller, & Rothman, 2020). Our conclusion, then, is that learners are working with an implicit system that does not resemble anything explicit that they might know, thus bolstering the idea that the development of that system involves implicit processes or learning.[10]

3.3 Language Is Learned Both Implicitly and Explicitly

We are now prepared to examine the third possibility: The linguistic system is learned both implicitly and explicitly. We have ruled out that explicit processes and learning can be involved in the acquisition of purely formal features of language as described in current linguistic theory. We also do not see how explicit learning can aid or somehow support the acquisition of such a system. But what about so-called surface features of language? These features include such things as noun endings, verb endings, articles, case marking, and other devices that indicate the language possesses certain abstract characteristics. To borrow from an example used in Section 3.2, rich verbal morphology in Spanish is a surface manifestation of the underlying properties related to TP, AGRP, CP (among others), and word order. Is explicit learning involved in the acquisition of such surface features?

It is our perspective that explicit learning is not involved – at least not in the traditional way such learning is conceived. That is, learners do not intentionally look for tense markers, person-number markers, mood markers, and so on as isolated aspects of language when processing input. Instead, as alluded to in Sections 2.2.1 and 2.3, such surface features are bound up with individual lexical items. In this view, learners do not explicitly (intentionally) learn that *-o/-oy* on the ends of verbs in Spanish is the surface manifestation of the features [+PRESENT], [+1st], and [−PLURAL]. Instead, learners accumulate scores of examples of verbs with this ending and enter them in the lexicon as full

---

[10] Staged development is well documented in L2 research and it all points to implicit learning from the outset. We only provide one example due to space limitations; however, the same kind of analysis we apply here can apply to such things as the acquisition of *wh*- question formation, the acquisition of negation, the acquisition of word order more generally, and morpheme orders, among many others.

morphophonological units with their meaning (e.g., *corro* "I run," *tomo* "I drink," *estudio* "I study," *vivo* "I live"). The internal mechanisms that organize and store lexical information create connections between these items such that *-o/-oy* is eventually linked to the underlying features of [+PRESENT], [+1ˢᵗ], and [−PLURAL].What learners may do, in some explicit way, is to try to figure out the meanings of things they hear (e.g., "Oh. That must mean 'I write'"). As meaning is mapped onto input strings, implicit learning is what (eventually) derives the grammatical properties of morphophonological units and links them to other components (e.g., syntax).

In short, we do not rule out the third possibility that both explicit learning and implicit learning are involved in L2 acquisition. Where we differ from other scholars (or perhaps try to clarify the debate in a way some have not previously envisioned) is that explicit learning can be involved in attempting to derive meaning during comprehension, but only implicit learning is involved in how the linguistic system is constructed over time. This is not a trivial distinction but is rarely, if ever, discussed by scholars.

4 Can Explicitly Learned Knowledge Become Implicit Representation?

A question that has been posed in the past is whether explicitly learned knowledge about an L2 can become implicit knowledge, or what we have called mental representation. We will touch on this only briefly here because the question has faded from most researchers' view. Stephen Krashen has long maintained that explicit knowledge derived from explicit teaching and learning ("learning" in his terminology) cannot become implicit knowledge ("acquired" knowledge in his terminology) (e.g., Krashen, 1982). For several decades, researchers argued this point, centering around three possibilities: (1) explicit knowledge can become implicit knowledge; (2) explicit knowledge cannot become implicit knowledge; and (3) explicit knowledge cannot become implicit knowledge but "somehow" it helps its development (i.e., there is an interface).

The first position has not fared well (e.g., Williams, 2009), largely because it is almost impossible with current tools to differentiate between whether explicit knowledge becomes implicit knowledge or whether learners simply get faster with explicit knowledge on the tasks used in the research, thus "masquerading" as implicit knowledge. At the same time, such a position has been undermined by theory and research on why explicit knowledge derived from explicit learning cannot become implicit representation, to which we now turn.

From a linguistic theory perspective, explicit knowledge cannot become implicit knowledge because, as Schwartz (1993) and VanPatten (2016) have pointed out, they are qualitatively different types of knowledge. There is no known mechanism in the human mind to convert explicit knowledge (whether taught or derived from one's own explicit learning) into the kind of abstract and complex mental representation we call language. Under this scenario, explicit knowledge derived from any kind of explicit learning resides outside of the implicit mental representation of language that learners create. They coexist in the mind/brain but are separate entities. We note that this is true of most conceptualizations of language, even non-generative ones (e.g., Ellis & Wulff, 2020; Sharwood Smith & Truscott, 2014). What is more, it is widely accepted in both linguistics and psychology that both explicit and implicit knowledge of language are not only qualitatively different but that they are stored separately in the mind/brain (e.g., N. Ellis, 2005; Williams, 2020).

The third position, perhaps the most popular among applied linguists and those involved in the research on instructed L2 acquisition, is that both explicit and implicit learning are involved in L2 acquisition. There are two perspectives on this. The first is that, although L2 acquisition is largely implicit as it is in L1 acquisition, because of well-worn L1 processing procedures (e.g., Herschensohn, 2010) and what is called "blocking" some aspects of the L2 available in the input aren't processed or incorporated into any mental representation and thus explicit learning can help. This is best articulated by Ellis (2015):

> In order to counteract the L1 attentional biases to allow implicit estimation procedures to optimize induction, all of the L2 input needs to be made to count … form-focused instruction can help to achieve this by recruiting learners' explicit, conscious processing to allow them to consolidate from-function bindings of novel L2 constructions. (p. 14)

This position makes sense as long as one takes a nonlinguistic approach to the nature of language. That is, the position assumes that language can somehow be presented to learners in ways that are usable in instruction. However, we know this is not the case. Any teacher of Spanish and French, for example, who has tried to give "rules" for the use of aspect in the past tenses has learned that what is provided to learners just can't capture what they need to actually develop aspectual distinctions. In fact, there is some evidence that doing this has the opposite effect; it can hinder acquisition (e.g., Rothman, 2008). And research on processability (e.g., Kessler, Liebner, & Mansouri, 2001; Pienemann, 1998) provides evidence that there are developmental constraints on what explicit learning can do to aid acquisition.

What is more, Ellis' claim lacks a mechanism by which explicit learning interfaces with implicit learning. That is, there is no specification of how the interface works. "Interface" is, at best, a vague construct, with little or no actual content. An example is illustrative. We examined two volumes, published twenty years apart: Ellis (1994b) and Rebuschat (2015). In neither book could we find a definition of interface. What is more, neither volume has this construct listed in the index, which is odd if there is some prevailing belief among researchers that there is some kind of interface between explicit and implicit learning. Along the way, there was a special issue of the journal *Studies in Second Language Acquisition* published in 2005 and dedicated to explicit and implicit learning. Again, we could not find a definition of interface in that volume. In short, the idea of an interface is, at best, vague and an actual definition may be elusive.

One way around this problem is to look at meaning versus formal properties as suggested by VanPatten (2015). There are surface features of language that are clearly linked to meaning, such as plural markers, certain case inflections, and certain kinds of verbal morphology, among others. Let's take a simple example. Pointing out to learners that *talked* means someone was talking in the past points the learner to how to interpret (i.e., make sense of) this kind of form when encountering it in the input. That is, *she talked* means something different from *she talks*. Explicit learning helps learners comprehend meaning, but the actual processing of the formal elements associated with that meaning will happen outside of awareness, that is, implicitly. In a nutshell, we believe it might be a fruitful avenue of theory and research to consider a bifurcation of the roles of explicit and implicit learning during L2 acquisition. One is relegated to one kind of thing and the other is relegated to something else. They don't really "interface" under this scenario. They may perform different roles and act on different kinds of linguistic elements (see also the brief discussion in Section 3.3).

5 But Wait . . .

In this section, we outline a number of issues that either support our previous conclusions about the primacy of implicit learning in language acquisition or may be considered as evidence to the contrary. We take each in turn.

5.1 Other Perspectives

As noted in Section 2, we take a generative perspective on the nature of language in the Chomskyan (Minimalist) sense. However, not all scholars do. It is beyond the scope of the present Element to examine in detail all the various perspectives, and here we will review the perspective that is most often juxtaposed to a generative approach: usage-based approaches.

Usage-based approaches (UBAs) refer to various accounts of language acquisition that hold two fundamental views. The first is that there is no special language-related module that guides acquisition. In particular, there is no such thing as Universal Grammar. The second is that language-related behaviors observed by users (L1 or L2) reflect a network of contingencies built up over time with exposure to language. For example, repeated encounters of the word *the* lead the network to posit that it will be followed by something like *woman*, *vice-president*, or *office* but never *swim*, *eat*, or *hang*. In everyday words, *the* is followed by something that is noun-like and not verb-like. In a sense, then, what generativists refer to as "phrases" and "phrase structure" are artifacts of the contingencies between elements that language users have encountered over time. Under such accounts, language is something that emerges in the mind/brain of the learner and consists of a vast network of such contingencies and even contingencies between contingencies (e.g., Tomasello, 2015).

Within UBAs, language is the result of the application of general learning and processing mechanisms to linguistic data. There is nothing "special" about language acquisition, and the abstract and complex aspects of mental representation noted by generativists do not require something like Universal Grammar to emerge. There is a complex and implicit mental representation within UBAs; it is just not one described by generativists. Within the last decade, some UBAs scholars have adopted construction grammars as a way to describe language (e.g., Ellis, 2013; Kerz & Weichmann, 2016). Depending on the scholar, construction grammars reflect form-meaning pairings including words, parts of words, phrases, and sentential structure such as passives (e.g., *The package was delivered by FedEx*) and ditransitives (e.g., *Megan gave the book to Bill*), among other constructions (e.g., Goldberg, 2003). The degree to which people generalize from the internalization of such constructions is a matter of debate among constructive grammarians.

The point to be underscored here is that, whatever perspective on language that UBAs take, it is not a classic Chomskyan account and certainly not a Minimalist account. In addition, Chomskyan approaches are concerned with what people know implicitly and these approaches use various methodologies to uncover such knowledge (e.g., grammaticality judgments, truth-value tasks, online processing such as self-paced reading and eye-tracking; e.g., White, 2020). As such, Chomskyan approaches are concerned with both what is possible and what is impossible in a given language. That is, all speakers of a language have implicit knowledge about what is not allowed (e.g., why contractions are prohibited in cases such as *Who do you wanna tell Bill the bad news?* and *Should I've done it?*; why we can't invert subjects and main verbs in English as in Spanish such as *Why eats Bill in that restaurant?* but

¿Por qué come Bill en ese restaurante?). Usage-based approaches, on the other hand, look at behaviors and what people do with language. As such, they are less concerned about what people deem to be impossible or disallowed in a language and focus on the "rules" that underlie what they actually produce (e.g., Roehr-Brackin, 2015).

Of concern here is where UBAs stand on the explicit and implicit learning of languages. To be sure, UBAs believe that resulting mental representation for language is implicit. The question is how such a representation comes to be. Although UBAs may not agree with us about the nature of language, they do agree (largely and in some cases fully) that language acquisition involves implicit and not explicit processes. A review of the literature and research within UBAs would yield the following two major tenets or conclusions.[11]

- Language acquisition is implicit. Explicit learning and explicit processing play little role in how mental representation develops over time.
- Language acquisition is input-dependent. Mental representation as exhibited in linguistic behavior evolves over time as learners are exposed to constructions, words, and so on, in communicatively embedded input.

A sample from a recent essay sheds light on these points:

> Despite the fact that many of us go to great lengths to engage in explicit language learning, the bulk of language acquisition is implicit learning from usage. Most knowledge is tacit knowledge; most learning is implicit; the vast majority of our cognitive processing is unconscious.
>
> (Ellis & Wulff, 2020, p. 77)

Although most UBAs centralize the role of implicit learning and processing in acquisition, some hedge and some even acknowledge a significant role for explicit learning – a kind of "having your cake and eating it, too" approach to the topic. For example, even though Ellis and Wulff lay the foundation for the centrality of implicit learning and processing in L2 acquisition, they go on to add that "Implicit learning would not do the job alone. Some aspects of an L2 are unlearnable – or at least are acquired very slowly – from implicit processes alone" (p. 78). What this suggests is that explicit learning can play a role in supplementing linguistic *behavior* but perhaps not tacit knowledge (see also Schwartz, 1993, who early on made a similar suggestion). It is not clear whether Ellis and Wulff would claim that explicit learning and processing are necessary. Our reading is that they would support the idea that it is supplemental or beneficial but under restricted circumstances.

---

[11] These two tenets are clearly not the only ones, but they are the most relevant for the present discussion.

In a similar vein, Roehr-Brackin (2015) makes the case for explicit learning and processing to play a role only when cognitive resources allow it. In this sense, she echoes Krashen's early claims that for the Monitor (explicit knowledge) to be useful, learners must have the time and resources to deploy it (e.g., Krashen, 1982).

> ... explicit processing is highly resource-intensive; accordingly, only so much explicit knowledge can usefully be handled at any one time by the human mind. In this sense, it can additionally be argued that when cognitive load difficulties arise, implicit processes may take over (again).
>
> (Roerh-Brackin, 2015, p. 131)

Of note here is that Roehr-Brackin is almost exclusively focused on visible performance (speaking and writing). Because UBAs are psychological frameworks, this makes sense. They are behavior-oriented in terms of the types of methodologies used to conduct research. In the studies she reviews, she notes that the deployment of explicit knowledge during performance is dependent on the type of "rules" under investigation, noting that research supports the idea that the benefits of explicit learning and knowledge tend to show up with constructions that are relatively high in schematicity and truth-value as well as low in conceptual complexity, for example (Roerh-Brackin, 2015, p. 129). In short, even with explicit processing examined only within the context of deployment of explicit knowledge during some kind of productive performance, there are limits to its usefulness.

On a broader reading of the literature with UBAs, our bottom-line take is that implicit learning is central to language acquisition in all contexts and that explicit learning is highly circumscribed by factors related to task and rule-type. Our speculation is that the research will demonstrate that, from the perspective of UBAs, the role of explicit learning in acquisition itself (and not performance on production tasks) will increasingly be relegated to a minor role at best. And, of course, UBAs continue to be challenged by the generativist arguments surrounding the problem of the Poverty of the Stimulus (POS). Certain aspects of language knowledge defy being explained by any kind of learning, explicit or implicit, and simply seem to emerge on their own or might have been present from the outset. We will delve into the POS question and its relevance to the explicit/implicit issue of acquisition in Section 5.4.

We would be remiss in this Element if we did not mention at least two perspectives that pull from a strong perspective of explicit learning as somehow central to language acquisition. One is sociocultural theory and the other is skill theory. Sociocultural theory applied to L2 contexts is concerned almost entirely with explicit learning; it simply ignores implicit learning and implicit knowledge in most of the research to date, centralizing explicit knowledge in the classroom context. In particular, it seems to focus on the kinds of rules and structures that classroom learners find in textbooks or even things that fall outside of the typical concept of language, such as sarcasm (e.g., Aljaafreh & Lantolf, 1994; Kim & Lantolf, 2018). Thus, it is difficult to discuss it in terms of explicit and implicit learning when the latter is absent from the framework to begin with.

Skill theory applied to L2 research has posited a role for explicit learning since its importation to L2 acquisition. The name most associated with this perspective is Robert DeKeyser. Early on, DeKeyser emphasized a fundamental role for some kind of explicit knowledge, especially in classroom settings (e.g., DeKeyser, 1995). Under skill theory, learners first have some kind of explicit knowledge about language (usually called declarative knowledge) that they then automatize over time through relevant practice. Under this scenario, explicit knowledge is essential for the acquisition of skill. We emphasize here *skill* and *not knowledge*, even though the theory makes use of terms like declarative and procedural knowledge, for example. As in the case of UBAs, the focus of skill theory is not what learners know implicitly but what they do automatically. This may seem a trivial distinction to some readers, but it is an important one. Skill theory does not, for example, concern itself with how learners come to know that particular structures are impossible, such as *Who do you wanna tell Bill the bad news?* and *Should I've done it?* It is only concerned with what shows up in learners' behaviors.

More recently, DeKeyser (2020) has suggested that implicit learning may play a role even under skill theory. He says, "Skill Theory by no means denies a role for implicit learning. There can even be a synergy between [explicit and implicit] learning for a particular rule or a distribution of roles between the two when a variety of different rules, patterns, or regularities need to be learned" (p. 96). DeKeyser does not specify what he means by "rules," "patterns," "regularities," or "synergy" and thus it is difficult to compare skill theory to other perspectives because others have much better defined and testable notions of what language as representation is. Our best guess is, based on various studies he and colleagues have conducted, that such things are to be found in the pedagogical grammars of language textbooks because these are the things for which learners are to develop some kind of skill (see, e.g., DeKeyser, 1995; DeKeyser & Sokalski, 1996; Li & DeKeyser, 2017).

To summarize and conclude this section, then, we note that different perspectives on the nature of language and what is measured (i.e., representation versus productive performance) may or may not lead researchers to posit implicit learning as central or perhaps to acknowledge its centrality while positing some kind of role for explicit learning. We have suggested that generative approaches and UBAs tend to align on the fundamental role of implicit learning in L2 acquisition, whereas other perspectives, such as sociocultural theory and skill theory, do not align. The debate, then, about explicit and implicit learning may in part be less a debate about learning and more about what researchers conceptualize as language itself and what is to be measured.

5.2 The Noticing Hypothesis

The Noticing Hypothesis (NH) (Schmidt 1990, 1993, 2001) proposed that learners have to notice forms in the input in order for them to be incorporated into the developing linguistic system. In Schmidt's (1990) words, "intake is that part of the input that the learner notices" (p. 139). Schmidt defines *noticing* as *focal awareness* on the part of the learner. Forms that are noticed are forms that the learner has registered consciously enough to report on them verbally. Noticing at this level indicates a level of attention that the learner has directed to a specific form, and it might also indicate a deeper level of processing. It is important to point out that noticing does not necessarily mean that learners have linked the form to a description or rule that corresponds to the form; just that they are aware of it on some level. Under the NH, forms that are available in the input but that the learner does not consciously register are not available as intake to the developing system. In other words, noticing is a necessary condition for intake and acquisition.

Schmidt's own experiences studying Brazilian Portuguese in Brazil form the basis of the NH. While he was in Brazil, Schmidt relied on a variety of resources to study Portuguese: he took formal Portuguese classes, kept a journal documenting his language-learning experiences, made a concerted effort to interact with native speakers, and recorded himself at roughly one-month intervals. Along with a colleague, he analyzed his output and compared the forms that he produced with the forms he commented on in his journal. They found that there was a relationship between availability and frequency of forms in the input and forms that Schmidt produced. Schmidt never produced forms that were not in the input, and he was more likely to produce forms that were frequent in the input. These two factors did not, however, explain when forms emerged in Schmidt's output. They also found that there was a relationship between when Schmidt commented on a form in his journal (i.e., noticed the form) and when it emerged in his output. Schmidt concluded that noticing a form in the input is necessary for converting input to intake. Once a form moves from input to intake, it is available for output. Once learners produce output that includes specific forms, these forms can be said to be acquired.

The NH has inspired a significant amount of research (see, e.g., the volume in honor of Richard Schmidt: Bergsleithner, Frota, & Yoshioka, 2013), and it is the basis for pedagogical interventions such as Focus on Form and certain kinds of Input Enhancement. In part because *noticing* as a construct is difficult to operationalize, the NH has been adapted and applied in different ways since its inception. In particular, it has been connected to the Output Hypothesis. Swain and Lapkin (1995) posited that output might help learners "notice the gap" between the L2 input and their developing systems, which is posited to promote acquisition. Similarly, it has been connected to the Interaction Hypothesis (e.g., Gass, 1997, 2003; Long, 1996), which states that interaction in communicative contexts, and specifically the need to negotiate meaning, facilitates the L2 acquisition process because it connects learner attention, language processing mechanisms, and input. Key to both of these hypotheses is the proposal that learner attention to input facilitates the acquisition process in important ways, usually because learners' attention is directed to the important features of the input.

Given this, it is worth considering in a bit more detail the relationship between input, intake, and noticing in Schmidt's formulation of the NH. Schmidt defines *intake* as the subset of the input that the learner *notices*. In other words, the sequence of acquisition goes something like this: exposure to input, focal attention on linguistic form, forms become intake to the developing system, forms are acquired. The strong version of the NH proposes that *no aspect of second language acquisition can be implicit or incidental*. Schmidt himself does not claim that learners must be aware of all aspects of linguistic form, so the strong version of the NH is not the one that its proponents defend. Instead, Schmidt leaves open the possibility that some aspects of language can be (and are) learned implicitly or incidentally but that some level of awareness is necessary for this learning to take place.

The weak version of the NH (and the version that most scholars accept to some extent) posits that some amount of learner attention facilitates L2 acquisition and that, if learners notice forms in the input, those forms may be more likely to become intake than forms that learners have not attended to in the input. In other words, most scholars would agree that some level of attention to the input is necessary for L2 acquisition, if only because input that is "tuned out" is not likely to become intake. That said, the strong version of the NH has come under critique on both empirical and theoretical grounds. The empirical critique is that there is a significant body of research demonstrating that L2 learners can and do acquire subtle properties of the L2 that are not available to them in the L2 input. This is the Poverty of the Stimulus problem, and we will return to it in Section 5.4. The theoretical objections are twofold. The first is that the NH is not founded on a clear theory of language, so it is not clear what, exactly, learners are noticing in the input. If the proposal is that learners notice the surface forms that correspond to underlying linguistic structure, such as subject-verb agreement or gender marking, that might be a matter of attention being related to form/meaning mappings. The issue is that the linguistic features that govern these structures – such as strong features for tense and gender marking – are not evident in the input. Instead, those features are acquired as a by-product of input processing in conjunction with learner-internal mechanisms. As other researchers (e.g., Truscott 1998; Truscott & Sharwood Smith, 2011) have pointed out, it is possible that Schmidt has the relationship between acquisition and noticing reversed. That is, it is not that noticing is a necessary condition for acquisition; rather, it is that acquisition is a necessary condition for noticing. In other words, once the form is represented in the developing system, it is available to the learner to reflect upon and to use in their analysis of the input to which they are exposed.

5.3 The Research on Implicit and Explicit Learning

In general, there are two main approaches to the relationship between implicit and explicit learning in SLA. The first investigates the relationship between classroom rules and what learners know and the second involves laboratory studies in which participants are exposed to a little bit of linguistic input (usually in the form of a semi-artificial language) and then tested on what they learned. The latter has its roots in Reber's (1967, 1976) early work on implicit and explicit learning, and it is the approach we will focus on here. There are a number of essays, book chapters, and volumes that provide overviews of research on implicit and explicit learning (see, e.g., Ellis, 1994; Rebuschat, 2015; Sharwood Smith & Truscott, 2014; Williams, 2009), so we will not replicate an overview here. Instead, we will examine the ways in which the constructs of explicit and implicit learning have been operationalized in laboratory studies and consider how this influences the way research has been conducted and what scholars claim to find. As such, we will limit our discussion to the assumptions and methodologies employed in laboratory studies.

As mentioned in Section 2.1, work on implicit and explicit learning has its roots in Reber's work on implicit learning in cognitive psychology. Reber operationalized implicit learning by testing participants' ability to judge whether strings of letters conformed to rule-governed finite-state grammars (see Section 2.1). He found that, after exposure to rule-governed letter strings, people were able to indicate whether new strings corresponded to the rule that derived the letter strings that people had been trained on. Crucially, the initial studies included no reference to rules and no indication in the instructions that people should search for rules. As Reber continued his work, he expanded it to include work on explicit learning. Reber (1976) operationalized explicit learning by telling participants that it might be beneficial to work out the regularities that governed the letter strings. Crucially, he did not tell people what the rule was; just that there was one that they should try to figure out. The participants in this study who were told there was a rule to work out performed poorly compared to the participants who were not told to figure out a rule. This provided some evidence that explicit learning, at least when it is operationalized as "these are rule-governed letter strings; it might be helpful to figure out what that rule is", is not as reliable as implicit learning.

This way of operationalizing implicit and explicit learning has largely been adopted in the field of SLA (except in instructed SLA research, where explicit learning is largely operationalized as providing learners with rules or regularities prior to some kind of practice or exposure), and the underlying assumptions have not really been questioned. Implicit learning is often thought of as "learning in the absence of awareness," where "awareness" is defined as the conscious focus on rules and regularities of the system and explicit learning is usually defined as "learning with awareness" (again, see Section 2.1). In other words, implicit learning is thought to have taken place when participants indicate some knowledge of structural regularities without explicit attention to those regularities. John Williams and his colleagues have conducted a series of studies that have investigated whether people can learn languages implicitly using a variety of grammatical structures and systems. All of these studies follow the same basic design: Participants are exposed to a training session that includes the target structures and are then tested in a follow-up session that includes a mix of items on which participants had been trained, as well as a mix of items on which participants had not been trained. In each of these studies, the training materials are constructed so that most of the vocabulary is in English and the structure(s) in question is not English. In some cases, the structures are novel vocabulary words that are created for the study, and in other cases, the structures are taken from a language that is not English. We illustrate in the following examples.

Leung and Williams (2012) investigated whether form-meaning mappings could be learned implicitly and, specifically, whether some mappings were easier to learn than other mappings. They did this using an artificial determiner system that consisted of two binary dimensions that resulted in a four-way distinction: animate/inanimate and near/far. Participants were told that the artificial determiners *gi* and *ul* were used with nouns that were close to the speaker and that the artificial determiners *ne* and *ro* were used with nouns that were far from the speaker. Participants were not told that *gi* and *ro* were used for animate nouns and that *ul* and *ne* were used for inanimate nouns. In other words, they were not told that an animate noun close to the speaker should be preceded by *gi* and not *ul* and that an animate noun far from the speaker should be preceded by *ro*. Participants completed an exposure session in which they were presented with a picture and the noun-article sequence that described the picture. For example, one trial showed a bull in the far corner of the screen, and this was accompanied by the description "ro bull." Another trial showed a picture of a telephone in the front corner of the screen, and this picture was accompanied by the description "ul telephone." The training block consisted of these pictures and accompanying audio descriptions, and participants had to indicate, after each trial, whether the picture was animate or inanimate. After the training session, participants completed a test where they had to make the same determination, but in this case the rules of the determiner system were violated. Reaction times were taken as a measure of implicit learning of the determiner system. Longer reaction times on ungrammatical sequences were taken as an indication that participants had learned the determiner system. The training and testing sessions were followed by a debriefing system in which participants were asked if they had noticed anything odd about the test sentences and, if so, what. They were also asked if they had noticed anything about the difference between *gi* and *ro* and *ul* and *ne*. Participants who had noticed differences in the usage of these determiners were classified as "aware" and participants who had not noticed any differences were classified as "unaware." A subset of their participants had noticed the difference between *gi* and *ro* and had correctly identified the animacy of the noun as the relevant factor that determined the choice of determiner, but the majority of participants (61 percent) had not noticed anything about the choice of determiner. Regardless of whether participants were classified as aware or unaware, they had slower reaction times and they made more errors when the relationship between animacy and article was violated. Leung and Williams interpret these results to mean that implicit learning of form-meaning mappings is possible.

Similarly, Williams and Kuribara (2008) investigated implicit learning of the head-directionality parameter. The head-directionality parameter refers to the relative order of phrasal heads and their complements. In head-initial languages, such as English, heads precede their complements, so that determiners precede nouns, prepositions precede noun phrases, verbs precede their objects, and, for functional items, complementizers precede tense phrases. In head-final languages, like Japanese, heads follow their complements, so that postpositions follow noun phrases, verbs follow objects, complementizers follow tense phrases, and so on. Williams and Kuribara created a semi-artificial language they called Japlish, which consisted of English words with Japanese word order and particles. Concretely, the sentence "Taro ate a strawberry" was presented to participants as "Taro-ga strawberry-o ate." In addition to basic word order, Williams and Kuribara included sentences that involved non-canonical word orders, such as OSV. These are possible orders in Japanese, such that a constituent can be moved to the left of the clause, usually for emphasis. For example, the sentence "Taro ate a strawberry" can be expressed with the SOV word order "Taro-ga strawberry-o ate," as above, or with OSV word order "Strawberry-o Taro-ga ate."

Williams and Kuribara used the same exposure/test-of-violations paradigm used in Leung and Williams (2012). The training set included several possible word orders, including simple canonical word orders with and without indirect objects, canonical word orders with embedded clauses, and non-canonical word orders with various constituents scrambled leftward. Participants were presented with each sentence orally and in writing and were asked to decide whether each sentence was plausible. In this case, the test of violations was preceded by an explanation of grammaticality and word order, and participants were then asked to indicate whether each sentence corresponded to their intuitions about what was grammatical in Japlish. The testing phase assessed participants' intuitions about the availability of scrambling in Japlish, and this section included scrambled sentences they had and had not been exposed to in the learning phase. Williams and Kuribara found that only a subset of their participants accepted scrambling as grammatical, even for structures they had been exposed to in the exposure task. The other participants seem to have imposed a strict SOV grammar on Japlish, rejecting anything that did not conform to SOV word order as ungrammatical. Williams and Kuribara also tested participants' intuitions about whether SVO (i.e., the dominant word order of their L1, English) is compatible with the grammar in the test sentences. Participants performed at roughly chance accuracy on these sentences. Williams and Kuribara argue that their results suggest that implicit learning is a stochastic process and that, especially given that participants did not reject the ungrammatical SVO word order a majority of the time, they had failed to reset the head-directionality parameter.

In general, research that has used this exposure/test-of-violations paradigm tends to find that participants do learn the "rules" of the system to which they are exposed and that they do so implicitly. They also tend to find that there is a tenuous relationship between knowledge of a rule and the acquisition of implicit knowledge. However, our argument is that, although these studies have a superficial resemblance to language-learning studies, they are closer to Reber's work on implicit learning and finite grammars than they are to being an accurate reflection of the processes involved in language acquisition outside of the laboratory. The assumption behind this particular type of input-treatment task seems to be that syntax is rule-governed and that the other components that make up the linguistic system, and particularly words and morphemes, are not as important for language learning as the underlying syntax. In other words, the assumption seems to be that vocabulary learning (or form-meaning mapping) is separate from rule-learning. This is out of step with what we know about the linguistic system and how language is acquired. As we discussed earlier (e.g., Section 2.3), language acquisition happens as a result of processing morpho-phonological units in the input for meaning. The mental representation for language develops as learners make form-meaning connections in the input to which they are exposed, and the developmental process is slow. The bulk of the research that has used this exposure/test-of-violations paradigm operates on an assumption that syntactic learning is divorced from morphophonological learn-ing, which is why studies such as Williams and Kuribara (2008) usually rely on using English lexis and grammatical structures from other languages or involve English lexis and an artificial determiner system, as in Leung and Williams (2012). The assumption that syntactic learning is essentially pattern learning and divorced from processing morphophonological units in the input has not, to our knowledge, been explicitly defended. In other words, one limitation of this research is that it is not clear what the learning gains in these studies reflect. They clearly reflect implicit learning of some sort – which is not surprising, given the body of literature in cognitive psychology that shows that people can learn patterns without attention and awareness – but it remains to be shown that they reflect *language* learning as we have defined language in this Element. Our conclusion is that they reflect pattern learning, which is the focus of a good deal of research in psychology; however, pattern learning and language acquisition are not equivalent and may not have much in common.

It is possible to use the same basic paradigm as the studies outlined in the three studies just described but to do so with an exposure task that involves basic input, including vocabulary, morphology, phonology, and syntax in the L2 – in short, real language that expresses some kind of meaning.[12] For instance, VanPatten and Smith (2015, 2019) investigated the acquisition of basic word order in Japanese and Latin. They provided participants with 100 sentences in either Japanese (VanPatten & Smith, 2015) or Latin (VanPatten & Smith, 2019) and relied on regular vocabulary quizzes to ensure that participants were processing for meaning. In both cases, participants were tested on basic word

---

[12] This argument was first articulated by VanPatten (1994): "To sum up, research from cognitive psychology related to attention and consciousness cannot speak to the issues of attention and consciousness in the acquisition of a natural language. The question of attention and conscious-ness in SLA must be investigated using the very languages that we teach and learn" (p. 31).

order and violations of basic word order in Japanese and Latin, and all participants in both studies were sensitive to the basic SOV nature of Japanese and Latin, indicating that they had reset the head-directionality parameter. In particular, in the 2015 study a significant group of learners projected beyond the kinds of phrases they were exposed to in treatment and showed sensitivity to violations of word order in functional phrases. The results of these studies are inconsistent with the findings reported in Williams and Kuribara (2008), who claim that their participants had failed to reset the head-directionality parameter. It is possible that the discrepancy between these two studies comes down to both the nature of the task and the input to which participants were exposed.

None of the studies discussed in the preceding paragraphs directly compared participants who had access to rules and participants who did not. Such a comparison is critical in order to determine whether explicit knowledge plays the kind of facilitative role in acquisition that proponents of a weak version of the NH and that proponents of a weak interface between implicit and explicit knowledge argue for. The studies that have done so have shown that explicit knowledge provides, at best, a marginal contribution, and, in some cases, it seems to actually make the learning process more complicated. (Later in this section we will touch on research on explicit and implicit teaching as it relates to this topic.) An early study example of this work is VanPatten and Oikennon (1996), which investigated whether explicit information was a necessary condition in learning to correctly interpret OVS word orders in Spanish. Spanish allows object-verb-subject word order in certain contexts and especially with clitic object pronouns, as in (7):

(7)   Lo ve María.
       him see.3sg.pres Maria.
       "Maria sees him."

English learners of Spanish tend to interpret these types of sentences as SVO sentences, so that the sentence in (7) is often misinterpreted as "He sees Maria." VanPatten and Oikennon compared a group of Spanish learners who received structured input with OVS word orders and no information about these OVS word orders to a group of learners who received the same structured input materials along with a short explanation of word order and the placement of clitic object pronouns. They found that the presence or absence of explicit information did not change whether learners were able to move away from SVO processing heuristics and toward correctly interpreting these sentences as OVS sentences. These results suggest that explicit information is not necessary for acquisition; the task was an offline task, so these results don't rule out the possibility that explicit information was helpful to learners in some way.

However, more recent research using eye-tracking (e.g., Wong & Ito, 2017) is suggestive. In Experiment 1 of that study, learners of French underwent treatment using processing instruction or traditional instruction focused on the causative with the verb *faire* "make," as in *Megan fait chanter une ballade à Bill* "Megan makes Bill sing a ballad." The issue was the same processing problem as in the above-cited VanPatten and Oikennon study, namely that learners mistake the first noun as the subject of the second verb and misinterpret the sentence as something like "Megan sings a ballad to Bill." Neither instructional group received explicit information or knowledge about the processing problem or the structure. What they found was that the processing instruction group's eye movements changed after treatment as they tended to look to the correct picture to match with what they heard but not the traditional group's movements. In short, with an online task, Wong and Ito demonstrated some kind of change that was not an offline task.

Also using online research methods, Andringa and Curcic (2015) used a semi-artificial language based on Esperanto to test whether the provision of explicit information would help learners process input more efficiently. Unlike the paradigm used by Williams and his colleagues discussed earlier in this section, Andringa and Curcic provided participants with input containing basic SVO sentences in Esperanto. All vocabulary was given in Esperanto, and they designed the input to include differential object marking (DOM), which is a property of Spanish in which animate direct objects are marked with the preposition *a* under certain conditions. Participants were L1 Dutch speakers with no prior knowledge of Spanish or Esperanto. Participants completed an exposure task that included fifty-two possible sentences for DOM; twenty-six of which contained animate nouns marked with the Esperanto preposition *al* and twenty-six of which contained inanimate nouns that were not marked. One group of participants received no information about DOM and a separate group of participants received explicit information about DOM. The treatment task was followed by a visual-world eye-tracking task that presented participants with an aural stimulus sentence and asked them to pick the picture that matched the last word in the sentence. Pictures were presented in pairs; half of the pairs included an animate and an inanimate noun, a quarter of the pairs included two animate nouns, and the remaining quarter of the pairs included two inanimate nouns. If participants had acquired implicit knowledge of DOM, they should have started looking at the animate noun in animate/inanimate pairs when they heard the *al*. Participants also completed an auditory grammaticality judgment task as a measure of implicit knowledge of DOM. Andringa and Curcic found that both the implicit and the explicit groups performed equally well in the picture selection task, but they found different patterns of looks toward the target noun in online processing. The implicit group showed a gradual increase in looks toward the correct picture. The explicit group showed a decrease in looks toward the target picture before they showed an increase in looks toward the target picture in the animate/inanimate trials. Neither group used the preposition *al* to predict the animate noun. The explicit group performed better on the grammaticality judgment task than the group that received input only. That the explicit group did better on the grammaticality judgment task isn't necessarily surprising; they had relevant knowledge they could apply, and grammaticality judgment tasks have been found to tap explicit knowledge when it is available (R. Ellis, 2005). The results of this study indicate that explicit knowledge changed online processing behaviors, but they don't demonstrate that having the rule helped learners rely on the presence of *al* for online processing. In this case, it seems like the presence of explicit information changed learners' processing heuristics but not in a way that allowed them to exploit the information in the input.

It is important to note, though, that in the Andringa and Curcic study, as in many of the studies that seek to explore explicit and implicit learning, there is the lingering problem of the nature of language. In their experiment, DOM was reduced to a simple rule of animate versus inanimate. But in languages such as Spanish, this is not how DOM works. There are subtle semantic and syntactic properties such that it is possible *not* to mark an animate noun with the preposition *a*, as in *Tengo una hermana* "I have a sister" and *¿Puedes recomendar un buen medico?* "Can you recommend a good doctor?" In addition, it is possible to mark inanimate nouns with the preposition *a* under certain conditions, such as *El carro sigue a la camioneta* "The car is following the van." In such studies, language is sometimes stripped of its natural properties for the purpose of laboratory research to create rules that are highly learnable explicitly. Yet, out of the laboratory, language is not stripped in the same way and is most likely acquired using implicit processes because of language's natural complexity and subtle, abstract properties. Given this, it's unclear how much the results of laboratory studies that strip language of its complexity for the sake of looking at the interface between explicit and implicit knowledge bear on the acquisition of language outside of the laboratory.

We would be remiss if we did not mention here research on explicit and implicit teaching, which is often conflated with explicit and implicit learning. In explicit and implicit teaching research, learners are either provided with rules prior to exposure/practice or aren't – and scholars often take the results of such research to draw conclusions about explicit and implicit learning, namely that explicit teaching (providing rules) is superior to implicit teaching (and thus explicit learning is better than implicit learning). Such research is summarized in meta-analyses such as Spada and Tomita (2010) and Goo et al. (2015), so we won't summarize it here. However, most of this research is questionable on methodological grounds. As noted, the language used in these studies is often stripped of its natural properties and/or researchers find the most codable "rules" that easily lend themselves to explicit teaching. Just as problematic, though, is the criticism leveled back in 2003 by Catherine Doughty who pointed out that such research suffers from a bias toward explicit testing formats (Doughty, 2003). That is, the measures used to assess learner knowledge tend to be those that invite the application of explicit knowledge while taking the test. In short, if you bias for explicit knowledge in your assessment of learner behavior and/or knowledge, then you will get results suggesting explicit learning is better than implicit learning.

In sum, the research on implicit and explicit learning has found that implicit learning is possible across a wide range of structures and methodologies, lending support to the proposal that language acquisition is primarily implicit in nature. It has also found that implicit learning can (and does) take place in the absence of explicit rules. What is more, research cited to support an important role for explicit learning is questionable on two fronts: the nature of language used in the research and the methodology and/or measures used to assess learner knowledge. To date, there is no strong evidence in favor of the proposal that explicit knowledge facilitates the acquisition of implicit knowledge, at least of morphosyntax, and there is no evidence that we can find that suggests it is necessary (cf. Leow, 2015). This does not mean that learners don't engage in explicit processes when they are interacting with input; as discussed in Section 4, it is likely that at least some aspects of vocabulary learning, for example, are (or can be) explicit.

5.4 The Poverty of the Stimulus Issue

Poverty of the Stimulus (POS) is traceable to Chomsky (1980), where he argues that the mental representation of language that speakers arrive at is underdetermined by the input they are exposed to. Put in simpler terms, L1 acquisition results in implicit knowledge that can't have been learned from the input alone and certainly isn't taught in any way. Here is a classic example. Speakers of English learn from the input that contraction is allowable, as in the following:

(8)   Do you want to go? ➔ Do you wanna go?

(9)   I have done it ➔ I've done it.

(10)   Who do you want to invite? ➔ Who do you wanna invite?

These are learnable because there are readily available data in the input for creating a "rule" of contraction. At the same time, speakers of English come to know that contraction is disallowed in the following sentences. That is, they are not permissible contractions.

(11)   Should I have done it? ➜ *Should I've done it?

(12)   Who do you want to talk to Bill about this? ➜ *Who do you wanna talk to Bill about this?

According to generative accounts, (11) and (12) are not allowed because there is a hidden trace (t) from the movement of a constituent and that trace blocks contraction.

(13)   I should have done it ➜ Should$_i$ I t_i have done it.

(14)   You want who to talk to Bill about this? ➜ Who$_i$ do you want t_i to talk to Bill about this?

Under the POS problem, how do speakers come to know that examples like (13) and (14) are not allowed when they aren't taught this and that the only evidence in the input is what is allowed? Somehow, the speaker of English has to arrive at some implicit knowledge of traces and that traces block contraction. But how do people come to know that traces exist if all they hear are allowable sentences with *wanna* and *I've*, for example? The conundrum is this: It's easy to arrive at what is grammatical because there is evidence of that in the input,[13] but a person also has to arrive at what is ungrammatical and sometimes (if not often) there is no evidence of that in the input because input only contains what linguists call *positive* data.

Second language learners are no different from L1 learners and speakers in that they, too, are confronted with the POS problem (e.g., Schwartz & Sprouse, 2000). They must arrive at not only what is possible but what is impossible – and this problem exists irrespective of their L1. For example, both Chinese speakers (whose L1 doesn't allow *wh-* constituents to move) and Spanish speakers (whose L1 does allow *wh-* constituents to move) must arrive at the impossibility of something like *Who do you wanna talk to Bill about this?* when neither language has contractions like English. And the research shows that they do.

The POS is a problem for explicit learning. The mental representation of an L2 learner has to "solve" the POS problem and must do so outside of awareness.

---

[13] It is possible to arrive at what is grammatical without having been exposed to something. This is another type of POS situation. We sketch this elsewhere in this section when discussing VanPatten and Smith (2015).

That is, implicitly within the developing system, abstract knowledge about traces is triggered so that L2 learners arrive at the impossibility of (11) and (12). This is not something that ever happens explicitly. Learners do not have conscious knowledge about traces and then apply that conscious knowledge somehow in learning.

There is another type of POS problem that we sometimes see in the L2 literature and that is when learners project early on from one type of datum encountered in the input to other related parts of the system even when they haven't encountered the latter in the input. This must happen implicitly. Such a phenomenon has been shown in VanPatten and Smith (2015). In that study, we tested whether learners of Japanese L2 (English L1) could project from a limited exposure to phrase structure to parts of the grammar they had not been exposed to in the input. English is a head-initial language, such that all phrases (e.g., NP, VP, PP, CP) follow the order X + complement, where X is the head. Japanese is head-final such that the configuration is always complement + X. Thus, English PPs are *in + the house, for + the people*, but such phrases in Japanese would be in the reverse order (e.g., *house + in, people + for*). In the VanPatten and Smith study, learners with no knowledge of Japanese or any other head-final language were exposed to 100 sentences in a picture task. Sentences were structurally simple and confined to instances of VPs and PPs, that is, two kinds of lexical phrases. Crucially, no sentences contained data regarding the structure of CPs (a functional phrase) with polar questions and embedded clauses. After exposure, the learners were given a surprise self-paced reading test in which they read both grammatical and ungrammatical sentences. The ungrammatical sentences followed head-initial order. However, the surprise test also contained sentences with CP elements to which they were not exposed. Those consisted of polar questions and embedded clauses, again consisting of both grammatical and ungrammatical word orders. Slowing down during reading at key points would be an indication that learners "detected" something funny about the sentence, even though they were focused on meaning (i.e., after each sentence, they had to answer a content question about what they'd just read). What we found was that a significant number of participants projected beyond the VP and PP structures they were exposed to and slowed down at key points in the polar questions. Another smaller group also projected even further and slowed down at key points when reading ungrammatical embedded clauses. Crucially, the ungrammaticalities had to do with the use of head-initial phrasing as opposed to head-final phrasing. What the results suggested was that learners could project beyond what they are initially exposed to, thus unconsciously expecting all phrase structure in Japanese to be head-final, even functional phrases such as CPs. In short, they projected from lexical phrases (VP, PP) to functional phrases

(CP). This study represents another kind of POS situation: learners coming to know more than what they are exposed to and that such knowledge must come about implicitly. Critical to the study was that no explicit teaching or learning was part of the treatment. Learners were simply exposed to sentences while engaged in picture matching based on what they heard as part of "learning Japanese."

There is yet another type of POS situation that speaks to the implicit learning of language and is evident in staged development. As an example, we will take early-stage acquisition of Spanish described in Section 3.2 and review it here. Research has shown that, at the beginning, Spanish L2 grammars are marked by a number of features, two of which we illustrate here. The first is that sentences tend to be copula-less and auxiliary-less regarding the Spanish equivalents of English *be*. In the examples that follow, learners simply omit such verbs.

(15)   *Juan alto* for *Juan es alto* "John is tall"

(16)   *Ella no aquí* for *Ella no está aquí* "She's not here"

(17)   *El chico corriendo* for *El chico está corriendo* "The boy is running"

We now turn attention to lexical verbs. During this early stage, learners also tend toward the default bare form that lacks any surface features. Spanish is a morphologically rich language with unique person-number endings. In the examples that follow, learners show a tendency to resort to a featureless verb rather than an inflected verb.[14]

(18)   *Yo estudia mucho* for *Yo estudio mucho* "I study a lot"

(19)   *Mis amigos vive cerca* for *Mis amigos viven cerca* "My friends live close by"

Both English and Spanish are finite languages, meaning they carry tense features on verbs. Yet learners in early-stage Spanish with English L1 are creating a tenseless system. That is, the absence of copulars and auxiliaries is indicative of no tense because one of their major functions in sentences is to carry tense information and mark the clause as finite. Likewise, the use of bare and featureless lexical verbs as in (18) and (19) also indicates a tenseless system. The question, then, is how does a tenseless system show up in early-stage acquisition when (1) the L1 has Tense as a feature and (2) the input in the L2 is replete with tensed and finite clauses? What is more, L2 learners of

---

[14] Teachers of Spanish typically categorize the bare verbs such as *estudia* and *vive* as third-person singular, as though these features are attached to the verb somehow. However, for languages like Spanish, there is no such set of features and the bare verb form, because it is featureless, steps in to "fill the gap" for this particular person-number combination.

Spanish are explicitly taught about and engage in practice with copular verbs, auxiliaries, and tensed verbs, yet these tend not to show up in spontaneous speech and in particular kinds of measurements that try to tap representation (e.g., self-paced reading) in early-stage learners. It appears that such learners are unconsciously creating a representation in which tense is absent in spite of explicit learning to do otherwise – and they are showing knowledge that is not represented in the input data they are exposed to and that knowledge developed implicitly.

To be clear, we are not saying that POS situations involve implicit learning in the sense that something in the input is processed implicitly. What we are saying is that POS situations are a result of implicit internal processes in which something universal about language interacts with something that has been processed in the input. In the case of contractions in English, learners process *wanna* and *I've* in the input. These data then "trigger" something internal that says something like "This language has contractions. Be sure not to contract across a trace." It's this latter part of the POS that must be entirely implicit in nature.

Overall, the POS situation is a problem for proponents of explicit learning and processing in L2 acquisition. Learners create mental representation in spite of explicit learning and processing and they also do so in the absence of data in the input (or the presence of data in the example of Spanish early-stage L2). And at least one study has shown that the explicit teaching of an abstract feature of syntax to learners (i.e., inverse scope) does not lead to projection to other aspects of scope (Wu & Ionin, 2021). To be sure, there have been arguments against the POS situation being real or observable (e.g., Dabrowska, 2015; Pullum & Scholz, 2002) and there are L2 scholars who simply don't believe it exists or ignore it (see, e.g., some of the chapters in VanPatten, Keating, & Wulff, 2020). Some scholars have attempted to explain POS situations via general (but innate) learning mechanisms, but learning is still largely or exclusively implicit under these scenarios (e.g., Goldberg, 2016; Perfors, Tenenbaum, & Regier, 2011). Our perspective is that the POS has survived attacks and is a challenge to various accounts of L2 acquisition (e.g., Schwartz & Sprouse, 2013). It is certainly something that proponents of explicit learning in L2 acquisition have yet to engage in any meaningful way (see, e.g., VanPatten, 2017).

6 Concluding Remarks

In this Element, we have argued for the primacy of implicit learning in L2 acquisition, relying on both theoretical and empirical sources. In addition, we have argued that explicit learning may certainly play a role (and most likely does) in L2 acquisition but not in the way traditionally envisioned. It would be easy for a reader to see our arguments as dismissive of certain positions, but it is not our intent to provide an overview of the research and critically examine it in what one might construe as a *review of the literature* or even a *state of the science*. Instead, we have made our biases about the nature of language up front along with the consequences of viewing language in this way. At certain points, we have made reference to alternative positions, arguing that how one views language may or may not influence one's perspective on the fundamental role of implicit learning. We have also reminded the reader of critical research on such things as staged development and ordered development that provide clear clues as to the implicit nature of what is developing in the learner's mind. Our hope is that, by taking the stand we have in this Element, we will push the field to engage in better discussion about the nature of constructs and to see that the implicit/explicit learning issue is not relegated to current empirical approaches in laboratories but must involve a triangulation of data accumulated across a broader spectrum of L2 research along with critical discussion about the nature of language itself.

Along this vein, we note that recent research in the construct of aptitude, for example, has now turned its attention to the role of implicit learning. Work by Gisela Granena and others has developed the construct of implicit language aptitude (Granena, 2020). The idea behind this approach is that traditional notions of aptitude are related to explicit learning only and have not adequately accounted for individual differences in rate of acquisition and ultimate attainment. The only way to account for such differences is to take a closer look at implicit learning. We take this turn in aptitude research as further evidence that implicit learning is central to acquisition.

It is not the intent of the present Element to make claims about pedagogical approaches or to support one approach over another. Practitioners often make curricular decisions independent of what the research says about L2 acquisition or they may be selective about research in order to bolster one approach over another. One could conclude, based on our arguments, that the research supports non-structural, non-grammar-based approaches to teaching because, in the end, explicit teaching and learning don't seem to be driving forces in acquisition. One could also conclude, however, that there are reasons unrelated to the research for the inclusion of explicit teaching and learning – reasons that go beyond the scope of the present Element (e.g., explicit knowledge is useful for editing written work; grammar learning makes adults "feel good"; strategy learning for communication may be useful). In a different vein, one could conclude that, at this point in time, the evidence does seem to favor implicit learning but that perhaps in the future we would see much more solid evidence favoring at least some kind of explicit learning for some things, so it might be premature to draw any pedagogical conclusions. And, of course, practitioners may make decisions based on social and circumstantial pressures that have nothing to do with acquisition (e.g., preparing students for particular kinds of standardized tests; demonstrating lesson and curricular objectives and progress to administrators). For all of these reasons, we leave ideas about curriculum development to practitioners and draw no conclusions on their behalf here.

We return now to the fundamental question that has driven much of L2 research for some time, whether scholars are aware of it or not: To what extent are L1 and L2 acquisition similar? Research on the explicit and implicit issue points to at least some similarity in that the evolution of a linguistic system as mental representation is almost exclusively implicit in nature. Any differences observed in L1 and L2 acquisition regarding the formal properties of language, then, are due to factors outside of the realm of implicit learning (e.g., language transfer and contact; access to and interaction with quality input; motivation and social factors). Implicit learning, at this point in time, seems to be central to language acquisition regardless of context or age.

References

Alemán Bañón, J., Miller, D., & Rothman, J. (2020). Examining the contribution of markedness to the L2 processing of Spanish person agreement: An event-related potentials study. *Studies in Second Language Acquisition*, 43 (4), 699–728.

Aljaafreh, A. & Lantolf, J. P. (1994). Negative feedback and regulation in second language learning in the zone of proximal development. *The Modern Language Journal*, 78 (4), 465–483.

Andringa, S. & Curcic, M. (2015). How explicit knowledge affects online L2 processing: Evidence from differential object marking acquisition. *Studies in Second Language Acquisition*, 37 (2), 237–268.

Bergsleithner, J. M., Frota, S. N., & Yoshioka, J. K., eds. (2013). *Noticing and Second Language Acquisition: Studies in Honor of Richard Schmidt*. Honolulu, HI: The National Foreign Language Resource Center.

Boeckx, C., ed. (2011). *The Oxford Handbook of Linguistic Minimalism*. Oxford: Oxford University Press.

Carnie, A. (2011). *Modern Syntax: A Coursebook*. Cambridge: Cambridge University Press.

Chomsky, N. (1980). On cognitive structures and their development: A reply to Piaget. In M. Piattelli-Palmarini, ed., *Language and Learning: The Debate between Jean Piaget and Noam Chomsky*. Cambridge, MA: Harvard University Press, pp. 35–54.

Dabrowska, E. (2015). What exactly is Universal Grammar and has anyone seen it? *Frontiers in Psychology*, 23 (June). https://doi.org/10.3389/fpsyg.2015.00852

DeKeyser, R. M. (1995). Learning second language grammar rules: An experiment with a miniature linguistic system. *Studies in Second Language Acquisition*, 17 (3), 397–410.

DeKeyser, R. M. (2003). Implicit and explicit learning. In C. J. Doughty and M. H. Long, eds., *The Handbook of Second Language Acquisition*. Oxford: Blackwell, pp. 313–348.

DeKeyser, R. M. (2020). Skill acquisition theory. In B. VanPatten, G. D. Keating, and S. Wulff, eds., *Theories in Second Language Acquisition*. New York: Routledge, pp. 83–104.

DeKeyser, R. M. & Sokalski, K. J. (1996). The differential role of comprehension and production practice. *Language Learning*, 46 (4), 613–642.

Doughty, C. (2003). Instructed SLA: Constraints, compensation, and enhancement. In C. Doughty and M. H. Long, eds., *The Handbook of Second Language Acquisition*. Oxford: Blackwell, pp. 256–310.

Ellis, N. (1994a). Implicit and explicit language learning: An overview. In N. Ellis, ed., *Implicit and Explicit Learning of Languages*. London: Academic Press, pp. 1–31.

Ellis, N., ed. (1994b). *Implicit and Explicit Learning of Languages*. London: Academic Press.

Ellis, N. (2005). At the interface: Dynamic interactions of explicit and implicit language knowledge. *Studies in Second Language Acquisition*, 27 (2), 305–352.

Ellis, N. (2013). Frequency-based accounts of second language acquisition. In S. M. Gass and A. Mackey, eds., *The Routledge Handbook of Second Language Acquisition*. New York: Routledge, pp. 193–210.

Ellis, N. (2015). Implicit AND explicit language learning: Their dynamic interface and complexity. In P. Rebuschat, ed., *Implicit and Explicit Learning of Languages*. Amsterdam: John Benjamins, pp. 3–23.

Ellis, N. & Wulff, S. (2020). Usage-based approaches to L2 acquisition. In B. VanPatten, G. D. Keating, and S. Wulff, eds., *Theories in Second Language Acquisition*. New York: Routledge, pp. 63–82.

Ellis, R. (2005). Measuring implicit and explicit knowledge of a second language: A psychometric study. *Studies in Second Language Acquisition*, 27 (2), 141–172.

Gass, S. (1997). *Input, Interaction, and the Second Language Learner*. Mahwah, NJ: Lawrence Erlbaum Associates.

Gass, S. (2003). Input and interaction. In C. Doughty and M. Long, eds., *The Handbook of Second Language Acquisition*. Oxford: Basil Blackwell, pp. 224–255.

Goldberg, A. E. (2003). Constructions: A new theoretical approach to language. *Trends in Cognitive Sciences*, 7 (5), 219–224.

Goldberg, A. E. (2016). Subtle implicit language facts emerge from the functions of constructions. *Frontiers in Psychology*, 28 (January). https://doi.org /10.3389/fpsyg.2015.02019

Goo, J., Granena, G., Yilmaz, Y., & Novella, M. (2015). Implicit and explicit instruction in L2 learning: Norris and Ortega (2000) revisited and updated. In P. Rebuschat, ed., *Implicit and Explicit Learning of Languages*. Amsterdam: John Benjamins, pp. 443–482.

Granena, G. (2020). *Implicit Language Aptitude*. Cambridge: Cambridge University Press.

Herschensohn, J. (2010). *The Second Time Around*. Cambridge: Cambridge University Press.

Hornstein, N., Nunes, J., & Grohmann, K. K. (2005). *Understanding Minimalism*. Cambridge: Cambridge University Press.

Hulstijn, J. (2005). Theoretical and empirical issues in the study of implicit and explicit second-language learning. *Studies in Second Language Acquisition*, 27 (2), 129–140.

Kerz, E. & Weichmann, D. (2016). Second language construction learning: Investigating domain-specific adaptation in advanced L2 production. *Language and Cognition*, 8 (4), 533–565.

Kessler, J.-U., Liebner, M., & Mansouri, F. (2001). Teaching. In M. Pienemann and J.-U. Kessler, eds., *Studying Processability Theory*. Amsterdam: John Benjamins, pp. 149–167.

Kim, J. & Lantolf, J. P. (2018). Developing understanding of sarcasm in L2 English through explicit instruction. *Language Teaching Research*, 22(2), 208–229.

Krashen, S. D. (1982). *Second Language Acquisition and Second Language Learning*. Oxford: Pergamon.

Leow, R. (2015). *Explicit Learning in the L2 Classroom: A Student-Centered Approach*. New York: Routledge.

Leung, J. & Williams, J. (2012). Constraints on implicit learning of grammatical form-meaning connections. *Language Learning*, 62(2), 634–662.

Li, M. & DeKeyser, R. M. (2017). Perception practice, production practice, and musical ability in L2 Mandarin tone-word learning. *Studies in Second Language Acquisition*, 39 (4), 593–620.

Long, M. (1996). The role of linguistic environment in second language acquisition. In W. Ritchie and T. Bhatia, eds., *Handbook of Second Language Acquisition*. San Diego, CA: Academic Press, pp. 413–468.

McCarthy, C. (2006). Default morphology in second language Spanish: Missing inflection or underspecified inflection? In C. Nishida and J.-P. Montreuil, eds., *New Perspectives on Romance Linguistics, Volume 1: Morphology, Syntax, Semantics, and Pragmatics*. Amsterdam: John Benjamins, pp. 201–212.

Perfors, A., Tenenbaum, J. B., & Regier, T. (2011). The learnability of abstract syntactic principles. *Cognition*, 118 (3), 306–338.

Pienemann, M. (1998). *Language Processing and Second Language Development: Processability Theory*. Amsterdam: John Benjamins.

Pritchett, B. L. (1992). *Grammatical Competence and Parsing Performance*. Chicago: University of Chicago Press.

Pullum, G. K. & Scholz, B. C. (2002). Empirical assessment of stimulus poverty arguments. *Linguistic Review*, 19 (1), 9–50.

Reber, A. S. (1967). Implicit learning of artificial grammars. *Journal of Verbal Learning and Verbal Behavior*, 6 (6), 317–327.

Reber, A. S. (1976). Implicit learning of synthetic languages: The role of instructional set. *Journal of Experimental Psychology: Human Learning and Memory*, 2 (1), 88–94.

Reber, A. S. (1993). *Implicit Learning and Tacit Knowledge: An Essay on the Cognitive Unconscious*. Oxford: Oxford University Press.

Rebuschat, P., ed. (2015). *Implicit and Explicit Learning of Languages*. Amsterdam: John Benjamins.

Roby, D. B. (2007). Aspect and the categorization of states: The case of *ser* and *estar* in Spanish. Unpublished Ph.D. dissertation, The University of Texas at Austin.

Roehr-Brackin, K. (2015). Explicit knowledge about language in L2 learning. In P. Rebuschat, ed., *Implicit and Explicit Learning of Languages*. Amsterdam: John Benjamins, pp. 117–138.

Rothman, J. (2008). Aspect selection in adult L2 Spanish and the Competing Systems Hypothesis. *Languages in Contrast*, 8 (1), 74–106.

Schmidt, R. (1990). The role of consciousness in second language learning. *Applied Linguistics*, 11 (2), 129–158.

Schmidt, R. (1993). Awareness and second language acquisition. *Annual Review of Applied Linguistics*, 13, 206–226.

Schmidt, R. (2001). Attention. In P. Robinson, ed., *Cognition and Second Language Instruction*. Cambridge: Cambridge University Press, pp. 3–32.

Schmitt, C. (2005). Semi-copulas: Event and aspectual composition. In P. Kempchinsky and R. Slabakova, eds., *Aspectual Inquiries*. Berlin: Springer, pp. 121–145.

Schwartz, B. (1993). On explicit and negative data effecting and affecting competence and linguistic behavior. *Studies in Second Language Acquisition*, 15 (2), 147–163.

Schwartz, B. & Sprouse, R. (2000). When syntactic theories evolve: Consequences for L2 acquisition research. In J. Archibald, ed., *Second Language Acquisition and Linguistic Theory*. Oxford: Blackwell, pp. 156–186.

Schwartz, B. & Sprouse, R. (2013). Generative approaches and the poverty of the stimulus. In J. Herschensohn and M. Young-Scholten, eds., *The Cambridge Handbook of Second Language Acquisition*. Cambridge: Cambridge University Press, pp. 137–158.

Sharwood Smith, M. & Truscott, J. (2014). *The Multilingual Mind: A Modular Processing Perspective*. Cambridge: Cambridge University Press.

Spada, N. & Tomita, Y. (2010). Interactions between type of instruction and type of language feature: A meta-analysis. *Language Learning*, 60 (2), 263–308.

Swain, M. & Lapkin, S. (1995). Problems in output and the cognitive processes they generate: A step towards second language learning. *Applied Linguistics*, 16 (3), 371–391.

Tomasello, M. (2015). Usage-based theory in language acquisition. In E. L. Bavin and L. R Naigles, eds., *The Cambridge Handbook of Child Language*. Cambridge: Cambridge University Press, pp. 89–106.

Truscott, J. (1998). Noticing in second language acquisition: A critical review. *Second Language Research*, 14 (2), 103–135.

Truscott, J. & Sharwood Smith, M. (2004). Acquisition by processing: A modular approach to language development. *Bilingualism: Language and Cognition*, 7 (1), 1–20.

Truscott, J. & Sharwood Smith, M. (2011). Input, intake, and consciousness: The quest for a theoretical foundation. *Studies in Second Language Acquisition*, 33 (4), 497–528.

Underwood, G., ed. (1996). *Implicit Cognition*. Oxford: Oxford University Press.

Vainikka, A. & Young-Scholten, M. (1996). Gradual development of L2 phrase structure. *Second Language Research*, 12 (1), 7–39.

VanPatten, B. (1994). Evaluating the role of consciousness in second language acquisition: Terms, linguistic features, and research methodology. *AILA Review*, 11, 27–36.

VanPatten, B. (1996). *Input Processing and Grammar Instruction*. Norwood, NJ: Ablex.

VanPatten, B. (2004). Input processing in SLA. In B. VanPatten, ed., *Processing Instruction: Theory, Research, and Commentary*. Mahwah, NJ: Erlbaum, pp. 1–31.

VanPatten, B. (2010). Some verbs are more perfect than others: Why learners have difficulty with *ser* and *estar* and what it means for instruction. *Hispania*, 93 (1), 29–38.

VanPatten, B. (2015). Foundations of processing instruction. *International Review of Applied Linguistics*, 53 (2), 91–109.

VanPatten, B. (2016). Why explicit information cannot become implicit knowledge. *Foreign Language Annals*, 49 (4), 650–657.

VanPatten, B. (2017). Situating instructed second language acquisition within second language acquisition: Facts and consequences. *Instructed Second Language Acquisition*, 1 (1), 45–59.

VanPatten, B. (2020). Input processing in adult SLA. In B. VanPatten, G. D. Keating, and S. Wulff, eds., *Theories in Second Language Acquisition*, 3rd ed. New York: Routledge, pp. 105–127.

VanPatten, B., Keating, G. D., & Wulff, S., eds. (2020). *Theories in Second Language Acquisition*. New York: Routledge.

VanPatten, B. & Rothman, J. (2014). Against "rules". In A. Benati, C. Laval, and M. J. Arche, eds., *The Grammar Dimension in Instructed Second Language Learning*. London: Bloomsbury, pp. 15–35.

VanPatten, B. & Oikennon, S. (1996). Explanation versus structured input in processing instruction. *Studies in Second Language Acquisition*, 18 (4), 495–510.

VanPatten, B. & Smith, M. (2015). Aptitude as grammatical sensitivity and the initial stages of learning Japanese as an L2: Parametric variation and case marking. *Studies in Second Language Acquisition*, 37 (1), 135–165.

VanPatten, B. & Smith, M. (2019). Word-order typology and the acquisition of case marking: A self-paced reading study in Latin as a second language. *Second Language Research*, 35 (3), 397–420.

VanPatten, B., Smith. M., & Benati, A. (2020). *Key Questions in Second Language Acquisition: An Introduction*. Cambridge: Cambridge University Press.

White, L. (2020). Linguistic theory, Universal Grammar, and second language acquisition. In B. VanPatten, G. D. Keating, and S. Wulff, eds., *Theories in Second Language Acquisition*. New York: Routledge, pp. 19–39.

Williams, J. (2009). Implicit learning in second language acquisition. In W. Ritchie and T. K. Bhatia, eds., *The New Handbook of Second Language Acquisition*. Bingley: Emerald Group Publishing, pp. 319–355.

Williams, J. (2020). The neuroscience of implicit learning. *Language Learning*, 70 (2), 255–307.

Williams, J. & Kuribara, C. (2008). Comparing a nativist and an emergentist approach to the initial stage of SLA: An investigation of Japanese scrambling. *Lingua*, 118 (4), 522–553.

Wong, W. & Ito, K. (2017). The effects of processing instruction and traditional instruction on L2 online processing of the causative construction in French. *Studies in Second Language Acquisition*, 40 (2), 241–268.

Wu, M.-J. & Ionin, T. (2021). Does explicit instruction affect L2 linguistic competence? An examination with L2 acquisition of English inverse scope. *Second Language Research*. https://doi.org/10.1177/0267658321992830.

Yang, C. (2004). Universal Grammar, statistics, or both? *Trends in Cognitive Science*, 8 (10), 451–456.

Cambridge Elements ⁼

Second Language Acquisition

Alessandro Benati

The University of Hong Kong

Alessandro Benati is Director of CAES at The University of Hong Kong (HKU). He is known for his work in second language acquisition and second language teaching. He has published ground-breaking research on the pedagogical framework called Processing Instruction. He is co-editor of a new online series for Cambridge University Press, a member of the REF Panel 2021, and Honorary Professor at York St John University.

John W. Schwieter

Wilfrid Laurier University, Ontario

John W. Schwieter is Associate Professor of Spanish and Linguistics, and Faculty of Arts Teaching Scholar, at Wilfrid Laurier University. His research interests include psycholinguistic and neurolinguistic approaches to multilingualism and language acquisition; second language teaching and learning; translation and cognition; and language, culture, and society.

About the Series

Second Language Acquisition showcases a high-quality set of updatable, concise works that address how learners come to internalize the linguistic system of another language and how they make use of that linguistic system. Contributions reflect the interdisciplinary nature of the field, drawing on theories, hypotheses, and frameworks from education, linguistics, psychology, and neurology, among other disciplines. Each Element in this series addresses several important questions: What are the key concepts?; What are the main branches of research?; What are the implications for SLA?; What are the implications for pedagogy?; What are the new avenues for research?; and What are the key readings?

Cambridge Elements ≡

Second Language Acquisition

Elements in the Series

A full series listing is available at www.cambridge.org/esla

Printed in the United States
by Baker & Taylor Publisher Services